Want to Get the Most out of Life?

Want to Get the Most out of Life?

Pursue Your God-Given Purpose!

Glenn Goree

RESOURCE *Publications* • Eugene, Oregon

WANT TO GET THE MOST OUT OF LIFE?
Pursue Your God-Given Purpose!

Copyright © 2021 Glenn Goree. All rights reserved. Except for brief quotations in critical publications or reviews, no part of this book may be reproduced in any manner without prior written permission from the publisher. Write: Permissions, Wipf and Stock Publishers, 199 W. 8th Ave., Suite 3, Eugene, OR 97401.

Resource Publications
An Imprint of Wipf and Stock Publishers
199 W. 8th Ave., Suite 3
Eugene, OR 97401

www.wipfandstock.com

PAPERBACK ISBN: 978-1-6667-1342-8
HARDCOVER ISBN: 978-1-6667-1343-5
EBOOK ISBN: 978-1-6667-1344-2

07/22/21

Scripture is taken from the Holy Bible, New International Version, NIV. Copyright 1973, 1978, 1984 by International Bible Society. Used by permission of Zondervan. All rights reserved worldwide.

To our daughter, Colleen Gwendolyn Lee, who is the bravest young woman I know. She nearly lost her right leg in a freak accident where she broke the tibia and fibula. During her lengthy recovery she had nine surgeries, had to drop out of nursing school, and lost her job. Several years later, she was diagnosed with breast cancer, endured six months of radiation therapy, and still suffers from the side effects of chronic fatigue. In both scenarios, she did not give up. She had been knocked down, but she refused to stay down. Although she endured unimaginable pain while her leg healed, she fought bravely and overcame. She completed her education and went on to become a nurse practitioner in psychiatry. Through all her trials, she found time to live and enjoy life, and is married to a great man.

"The *positive thinker* sees the *invisible,*
feels the *intangible*, and achieves the *impossible.*"

WINSTON CHURCHILL
(italics added)

Contents

Introduction | ix

1. Quest for Freedom | 3
2. Family Opposition to Developing Self | 21
3. The Role of Pastoral Employee Counseling | 49
4. God Made Mankind to Have Purpose | 71
5. How to Discover Purpose | 91
6. How to Pursue Purpose | 121

Introduction

Twelve years ago, I was blessed to contract as an Employee Assistance Program (EAP) onsite counselor for the third largest global bank. This financial institution has two principle call centers in the city where I lived. The total number of employees at these facilities exceeds five thousand. This number does not include an additional thousand employees who work at the bank's branch locations. In the following chapters, I reference people I counseled, but I've changed all the names for their privacy.

As time would show, the best advice I received on how to implement my job successfully came from my new boss. He provided the finest nautical analogy I have ever heard. He said an EAP counselor in a call center is like a chaplain on an aircraft carrier. As the years passed his words of wisdom proved true.

Here are some examples. The chaplain on an aircraft carrier and the counselor in a call center will, in the course of daily activities, randomly come across employees they have counseled. They bump into the sailors or corporate employees in hallways, onsite cafeterias, elevators, or stairwells. Sometimes the chaplain and EAP counselor may be invited to a management meeting. And whom do they see? A manager who perhaps just yesterday was crying in the counselor's office over a seriously troubled marriage.

In short, both the chaplain and the EAP counselor have a captive audience of several thousand employees. The chaplain and the crew are surrounded by water, while the EAP counselor and his fellow employees share a common sea of corporate employment.

Introduction

Needless to say, I knew none of these truths when I started. However, I did know I had been given the best opportunity I would have in my professional career. As I became more experienced and comfortable in my job, something unexpected happened. My role as a counselor grew and changed and morphed into that of a pastoral employee assistance counselor. In the confidential setting of my office, I found that many employees asked for a Christian-based approach to their problems. That is how, more often than not, my role became that of a Christian pastoral counselor.

Life can be either accepted or changed. If it is not accepted, it must be changed. If it cannot be changed, then it must be accepted.
WINSTON CHURCHILL

— 1 —

Quest for Freedom

THERE BEATS IN THE breast of every human being an inherent, God-given quest to be free, a quest that is at the core of the freedom of choice. Here is my definition of quest. A personal quest is a decision to embark on a life journey that initially only the quester believes is possible. The quester needs to carefully measure all the factors, good and bad, and calculate ways to ensure a successful outcome.

This quest for freedom is expressed from birth and continues until death. I further believe this quest for freedom is located in the heart, mind, soul, and spirit. Only God creates these parts of the human psyche which he gives to each fetus. I also believe this quest is part of our DNA, also created by God. Listen to David's words: "For you created my inmost being; you knit me together in my mother's womb. I praise you because I am fearfully and wonderfully made; your works are wonderful, I know that full well. My frame was not hidden from you when I was made in the secret place. When I was woven together in the depths of the earth, your eyes saw my unformed body. All the days ordained for me were written in your book before one of them came to be" (Ps 139:13-16).

The quest for freedom is exhibited at first in very simple behaviors, such as a baby's squirm, crawl, first steps, and learning to walk; a child's learning to run, engaging in sports, riding a bicycle, and joining the Boy Scouts; and later, an adolescent's completing high school. These behaviors evolve to more complex expressions such as joining the military, obtaining a formal education, dating, marriage, or becoming an entrepreneur.

As you can see, the quest starts as a newborn infant becomes a child, preadolescent, adolescent, young adult, adult, mature adult, and finally a senior. Each stage is the foundation of all behaviors, regardless of whether an individual is married or single, a parent or childless, employed or unemployed. Interpersonal and internal struggles are confronted in each stage—for example, insecurity, low self-esteem, poor self-image, fear of rejection, fear of failure, and so on.

We can compare our quest to the birth of a monarch butterfly. Have you ever watched a video of the butterfly's struggle to be born? The laborious fight to be free is fascinating to behold. The observer is often drawn to help liberate the butterfly from its cocoon. If you encounter this rebirth in real life, do not be tempted to help the butterfly. The struggle allows the wings to fully form and become strong. If you assist the butterfly, the wings will not develop correctly and the butterfly won't be able to fly.

A whole new dynamic becomes evident when two individuals decide to live together by marrying or cohabiting. Most couples will voluntarily limit personal freedom when they commit to a relationship. The reason for this voluntary limit of freedom is the belief that relationships will mutually improve the quest of freedom for both parties. I also think that when relationships are healthy, their quest for freedom is enhanced to a greater extent than before they entered the relationship.

However, not all couples will have a positive outcome to their mutual quest. Their common quest for freedom can become a conflict. The emerging fight is between what each individual self defines as freedom. The termination of the relationship occurs when one or both parties abandon the relationship. This inability to resolve the conflict caused by the quest for freedom is the cause of divorce, employment change, addictions, and other unresolved issues.

Throughout life, there is a constant seeking and searching for the balance of the self's and the other person's freedom. And because this balance is such an integral part of our DNA, it cannot be abandoned. Without this constant search for self in freedom until death, we cannot be who God fully intends us to be.

Couples who can resolve these conflicts grow in their desire to pursue a life epic. Let me define a life epic. The couple seeks to establish, maintain, and broaden their definition of what freedom has come to mean to them. This mission is achieved over their lifetimes. However, from the beginning of this quest there are speedbumps, stop signs, potholes, and a sinkhole or two. A life epic could be anything, such as becoming a doctor or traveling to Africa or Afghanistan. It could also be joining the Peace Corps, the military, or the French Foreign Legion.

How did I arrive at this conclusion? After thousands of hours searching the faces of employees who came to me as their EAP counselor, I concluded they all wanted the same goal; however, they weren't aware of it. In fact, I believe if I articulated my conclusion to them, each would deny it. Nevertheless, in their desire to be free from the pain brought on by broken hearts, fragmented souls, and shattered wills, I concluded their true pain was not in the brokenness. Brokenness was merely a symptom of much deeper pain.

I learned this truism as a combat medic many years ago in the Rhodesian army. Our instructor continually emphasized, "Don't get lost in the symptoms. Search deeper than the presenting symptoms and there you will find the malady." And this wisdom equally applied in mental health as well.

The clients' actual pain was that they had never started their personal, internal quest for freedom. What hindered their quest? They had never defined their freedom in the first place.

It would be like if you and a friend decided to take a ride in a vehicle. You start the engine, your friend hops in the passenger seat, and you take off down the road.

Your passenger asks, "Where are we going?"

"I don't know."

"Do you at least have a map?"

You reply, "No."

Want to Get the Most out of Life?

And then your passenger asks, "If you don't know where you are going and you have no map, then why are you driving the car?"

You shrug. "Seemed like the thing to do at the time."

I concluded that many employees I counseled at this facility were like these two people who jumped in the car. They were not sure where they were going and they possessed no life road map. Going out and getting a job seemed like the right thing to do at the time, but there was no forethought as to where their lives were headed—not because they were derelict in life planning, but because by the time they had reached an accountable age, they were full of inaccurate information about themselves. The idea of a quest was over before it started.

Many of the employees were young enough to be my children, and as a father and their counselor, their defeatist attitudes hurt me. They all had so much potential. In fact, I will go on the record to say they had great potential. Their problem was they didn't believe they had potential. I talked to young and old alike who could have been doctors, lawyers, mathematicians, nurses, career military officers, accountants, scientists, or professional diesel mechanics, or have excelled in many other careers. However, it didn't matter how much I demonstrated this through facts in their lives—they refused to follow the quest.

Let me qualify here and say that by no means was their current employment as customer service specialists beneath their dignity. What I and they could see was that they were round pegs in square holes. They were doing their jobs, but they were not happy because they weren't doing what they felt like they were called to do.

Quest for Freedom: Three Specific Examples

1. The Engineer:

    After I'd been in the job about six months, Brian—a middle-aged, married man between forty and forty-five—came to my office. His face had frustration written all over it. After he loosened up, he confided he had been in the call center for the better part of a decade, but hated it. He had only taken the job because he had to support his family. However, his kids were grown and had left home, and now it was just him and his wife.

Suddenly, I was inspired to ask him a question I subsequently asked many clients: "If you had a pot of gold to fund an education to be anything, what would that be?"

Brian squirmed a little in his chair and avoided eye contact. He was a big man, but my question reduced him to a schoolboy sitting in the principal's office.

He eventually replied, "I'd like to be a mechanical engineer."

I asked about his childhood. He had characteristics of someone with Attention Deficit Disorder but had never been diagnosed, and educational personnel had done little to assist him. He was exceptional in math and science but had earned low grades in the rest of his subjects and had a difficult time staying still and focused.

Brian loved to tinker with engines, so he ultimately became a mechanic, believing a college education was out of his grasp. His parents had offered no support. In fact, their attitude throughout his schooling was for him to learn to straighten up, do his schoolwork, and stop his fidgetiness in class.

I asked what he wanted out of our conversation. He wasn't sure, except he needed someone with whom he could vent. I then dropped a bombshell on him by asking why he didn't consider going to college to become an engineer. The expression on his face is difficult to describe. It was somewhere between shock and amazement. It was almost as though I had sucker-punched him in the stomach.

His immediate reply was, "I can't." He answered as though I were a fool to even suggest this idea. I replied that transferring to another job within the company was not the answer, and he agreed. I further pointed out that trying to get another job in the field of call center work at his age would be difficult. Even with his experience, his age was against him and besides, he would only be switching trains, not riding a new mode of transport.

Brian then gave me the rebuttal most of my employees spouted when I suggested returning to school or college: "I can't afford it."

I looked at him and said, "You can't afford *not* to do it." I let that sink in, then added, "First, a person has to decide on a quest, and then he goes out to find the money to do it. Otherwise no life decisions would ever be made. Don't you agree?"

He did.

I then proposed three scenarios. "You can attend school full-time and work at the call center part-time. Or, your wife can help out with finances and get a job outside the home. And thirdly, remember that when you finish your education, you will earn more money."

After a few seconds I added the clincher. "If you don't accept the challenge now, you will never know if you could have succeeded. In old age you will look back on your life with regret that you didn't try."

A couple more seconds. "Do you want to go to your grave having never tried?"

His head lowered and his shoulders sagged. Then he straightened, and the expression on his face changed. His eyes twinkled and he beamed.

I have seen this same expression on other employees' faces when they realized that the impossible could became probable.

Brian's final rebuttal was, "I'm too old."

I smiled and told him about a lady doctor I'd met in the ER at two o'clock one morning. She had been a nurse for many years and had gone through a divorce, but had finally decided to become a doctor at age forty. I met her ten years later, a successful MD.

That clinched it. He asked, "Can I bring my wife so we can discuss this with her?"

Quest for Freedom

After we made the appointment, Brian left my office like a schoolboy who had just made the dean's list. He almost skipped down the hall. Why? Because in his mid-forties he was finally going to begin his quest for freedom.

A week later, Brian and his wife came for their appointment. They had discussed my proposal at home and needed to visit me to confirm their decision. I can't recall how many years they had been married, but I am guessing at least twenty. So they knew each other's hearts well.

I reviewed my suggestions and witnessed a magical moment for them. It's not often that situations like these work out so well.

Brian looked into her eyes and asked, "You don't mind?"

Love shone from her face as she replied, "No."

For some reason, they accepted the decision because the meeting in my counseling office seemed to make it official.

They left the office like two high school sweethearts, with him jabbering away in his excitement and her arm around his waist in support. I never saw them after that day, but I know they both were starting their quest together for freedom.

Brian's quest may result in other positives. Firstly, when one person in a couple decides to start a quest and the marriage is sound, that person's spouse begins the same quest. Secondly, the beauty of these two questers is that they as one will blaze a trail in a new freedom neither of them had thought possible. And thirdly, in the toil, debt, late nights, term papers, final exams, living on peanut butter and jam sandwiches, this couple will be the happiest they have ever been in this autumn of their marriage.

As it will be the first time, he will actually be free. He will discover that thieves can take all he owns, but no one will be able to steal his newfound knowledge. Together, he and his wife will carve this freedom out of life when others say it can't be done.

Want to Get the Most out of Life?

2. The Pharmacist:

I will never forget the day I met Maria, a young African American girl about twenty-two. She had finished her corporate training and had been working as a call center specialist for only a few months. She came to my office because her live-in boyfriend was being physically abusive, he did not have a job, and he was seeing another girl on the side. To add to the problems, he had a child with another young woman who was jealous of these two living together. I told her to stand up to him by saying she would leave him if he didn't live up to his obligations.

Maria stated that she would follow my suggestions. I didn't see her for several months, and then she returned again to report that her boyfriend had straightened up and was working. He also was prudently limiting his time visiting his child and former girlfriend. Maria seemed happy, but neither of us was convinced his word was his bond.

Again, several more months passed and she came to see me again. When she sat down in my office, I could tell by her woeful expression that something terrible had happened. She stated that she hated her job but confessed this was not the reason for her visit. She was pregnant by this young man, who had not been consistent in his fidelity.

Maria had given him an ultimatum. Now that she was pregnant, he had to either fully commit to her or he had to leave and stay with his former girlfriend. As I learned in our last two visits, the mother of his child had been driving a wedge between Maria and her boyfriend. As of this visit, he had pledged to stay with Maria. During her pregnancy, I saw her several times because she had severe medical complications. There was a danger at one point during her pregnancy of losing her baby.

After her baby was born, Maria came by to give me an update on her relationship. The baby was doing well and her boyfriend was behaving himself. She guessed that having a child and her laying down the law to him had straightened him up to own his responsibilities. However, now that her life had seemingly settled down, she still was not happy with her job. I asked her the same question I had asked Brian: If she had a pot of gold and could return to school, what would she study?

I was amazed when she said pharmacy because I had no indication from her that she had an interest in math and science. She revealed she had been a straight A student through high school and that she had been accepted to one of the best colleges in our city that had a pharmacy program. Bewildered, I asked why had she not followed up on this offer. Her answer included excuses I've heard too often. There was no money, she hadn't received parental or family support, and higher education was not a priority in her family and they had not budgeted money for any of their children's formal education.

Like a P-51 Flying Tiger pilot during World War II, I nosedived into refuting these excuses. First: I vehemently stated that she had overlooked a fundamental principle in pursuing a quest. The decision to have a vision and a mission for her life must be decided first. And it was best to write it out on a piece of paper in outline form. Now that this vision and mission had substance, it gave her a detailed plan.

Second: After defining the quest, a person must then research ways to locate the funding and identify other resources to fulfill the vision and mission. By vision, I mean the dream to be a pharmacist, and by mission, I mean the plan with which to fulfill the vision.

Third: Maria had to ignore the lack of parental or family support. It is always the person with a quest and defined vision and mission who is viewed as a little crazy. She was the silent majority because she was thinking outside of the box in which her family had always lived.

We used my office computer and located the website of the original university that had accepted her out of high school. As is the case with most young graduates, finessing all the hoops of admissions to college was overwhelming. So in my office we navigated step-by-step how to proceed. We reviewed grants and loans and special funding for African American female students through the university. We also reviewed how to explore grants outside the university. She learned it wouldn't be easy, but that she could do it.

We discussed possible part-time work at the company, but if need be, she could also look for work with another employer. I also spoke from experience and added that once she was in the swing of returning to school, she would discover that her perceived problems wouldn't be as unsurmountable as she supposed. I explained that people she'd meet at the university would love to help a young mother fulfill her career dream. All of this was just a little overwhelming to Maria at first, but I could tell by the gleam in her eyes that she grasped and understood it.

We settled on a game plan. She was going to register for the pre-pharmacy program for the next school opening and begin the plans to engage in her quest. After that day I didn't see her again, but I learned she had resigned, and as far as I know, she is a pharmacist today.

3. The Nurse:

Carol came blazing through my office door like a meteorite. She was a young lady with a mission. As a side note, I had an open-door policy because the employees worked in shifts and had various breaks and different lunch times. Many employees dropped by without an appointment. They knew if the door was closed, I had an employee with me. Now back to Carol.

She immediately sat down in the chair in front of my desk and proclaimed, "I did what you said, Mr. Goree."

To be honest, I didn't remember what I'd told her and asked, "And what was that?"

"I realized if I want to go to nursing school, I have to make sacrifices in my life."

Bells rang, and I recalled our previous visit. "What did you do?"

Carol declared she had a very large electric bill plus a few other debts. She had sold her recently purchased plasma TV and used the money to pay off her credit cards. Now she was debt free except for monthly bills. Without taking a breather, she announced she didn't need satellite TV and had cancelled it. And although she loved her new car, she had retuned it and made the financial adjustments for a much smaller vehicle which lowered her monthly payment by half.

She finally declared, "These are all just things. Sure, I can afford them and although I like my job, I really want to be a nurse. I realize that I cannot let *things* get in my way. I decided to live on half of what I earn so I can pay tuition. I am going to enroll in the two-year program at a local community college to become a nurse."

During a previous visit when I learned she wanted to become a nurse, I'd asked what were some changes she could make to reach her goal. The conversation planted seeds about life choices. Those seeds germinated and grew, blossoming into her quest. I was impressed with all her decisions, but most especially with her willingness to trade in her new car and to drive a smaller one to cut her monthly payment in half.

She thanked me for my help and left my office resolute to work part-time and attend college. She was a single mother with little or no help from the child's father and was determined not to be dependent on anyone. Her departure was like a gust of wind in a meadow that swept away everything in its path, leaving a quiet stillness in its wake.

Quest Defined in Detail

What do you glean from these stories about the meaning of a personal quest?

When we typically think of a quest, we think of some pioneering character, such as Christopher Columbus sailing across the unknown Atlantic Ocean. Or Leif Erickson in Viking lore, who is thought to have discovered America long before Christopher

Want to Get the Most out of Life?

Columbus. Neither of these questers sailed the open sea without calculation, preparation, experience, and training. Their quests encountered obstacles of many varieties: rough seas, inhospitable land, and curious or warlike native inhabitants. They also faced unanticipated difficulties they could not prepare for but had to surmount as they occurred.

The employee on a quest will also encounter rough seas of a financial and human nature. For example, sad to say, sometimes family and friends will think the quest is a hopeless dream, and instead of offering encouragement, they will oppose or hinder the quest. Columbus encountered such opposition when he attempted to raise money for his quest and was denied many times by potential benefactors. However, he struck pay dirt when he finally sold Queen Isabella on the idea and she funded his quest. In like manner, our modern-day quester will also find the money day-by-day, week-by-week, or month-by-month to fund his or her quest.

I counseled many young adults like Carol who made a decision to change the trajectory of their lives and whose parents not only didn't support the quest, but refused to help along the way as a passive means of sabotaging the mission. Often times, this withdrawal of outside support had the opposite effect. Instead of discouraging the quester, the lack of support made her more resolute and determined to finish her quest without a disparaging family. Again, sad to say, the quester's relationships with family and friends was never the same afterward, as they each went their separate ways in life. In Carol's situation, the only exception to not associating with each other occurred when the family wanted to see the granddaughter.

You may wonder why some parents would not support their children or would even discourage them from seeking self-improvement. When talking with young employees who received no family support in their personal quests, I found two factors in common. First, the parents and family didn't have an education beyond high school, and advanced education seemed to have no value to them. Pursuing a higher education was fine for other people but not for their family. Their work ethic demanded that each child get a job after high school to produce another regular income to help the family pay the bills.

Second, though not often stated—but implied in a passive attitude—parents and/or family members were jealous of the adult child who wanted more in life. They felt this person was betraying them because the quester's education would lead to a better job, which in turn would lead to a better lifestyle. No one else in their family had achieved this higher standard; therefore, this achievement was a little outside their mindset of possibilities.

Carol knew about all these possible implications I have alluded to, plus she understood she had to make several personal sacrifices in order to achieve her quest. When I was young, we called it "tightening the belt." She would have to stay on budget each month. Her dietary habits would change to include more hot dogs and Spam. A treat she may have given to her daughter in the past would be given less often. She would also be forced to financially scale down even more, perhaps moving into a smaller apartment.

However, she knew that in the long run, the sacrifices she was making now would have both financial and personal dividends for her and her daughter in the future. She also knew the time it would take to achieve her quest—two years. Carol counted the financial cost and sold personal possessions, paid off bills, and determined not to accumulate more debt. In counting the cost, she also knew that when she became a nurse, she would earn more money right off the bat than she was earning in her current job.

What happened in Carol's life to move her from having a dream to taking action to fulfill that dream? I believe she was motivated by a unique internal spark stemming from a desire to improve her situation. In fact, it wasn't a spark but an explosion. It was the same type of spark that ignited Davy Crockett and Daniel Boone, explorers extraordinaire—the same catalyst that led to Lewis and Clark forming an expedition to explore the Missouri and Columbia Rivers to the Pacific.

This spark that leads to a quest has a *vision* and a *mission*. And in this next sequence of discussions we are going to explore the meaning of these words.

Want to Get the Most out of Life?

Quest Refined by Defining Vision

A quest vision is a picture in the quester's heart of the personal goal to be achieved. The image is crystal clear, bright, colorful, focused, and as real as the quester's pulse. The quester's problem is that no one else can see it.

Let's equate this vision to a six-foot rabbit friend named Hoppy who is dressed in a tuxedo. The quester, who I'll call Jeff, walks into a crowded room and introduces Hoppy to his friends. Remember, only Jeff can see Hoppy, therefore everyone else in the room thinks our brave soul is a bit touched in the head.

They cannot see Hoppy because each one, at a certain time in their lives, encountered a shadow of Hoppy, but the shadow was too scary for them to embrace in friendship. Some people in the room may have allowed Hoppy to enter into their lives for a few days, months, or years, but then gave up their belief in Hoppy because of peer and family pressure. To become an engineer, doctor, nurse, or lawyer—or a professional electrician, plumber, or welder—had been a silly dream. The peer pressure became too much for Hoppy to handle, so he took the hint and departed.

I believe that when someone like Carol declares she sees Hoppy and doesn't care if anyone else sees him or not, something dire happens to all the malcontents discrediting Hoppy. His ghost hovers over each person in the room who once believed in him but succumbed to pressure. The death of their quests leaves a deep-seated, suppressed bitterness that accumulates over the years. Although these naysayers move on in life, a residual germ of disappointment remains which stings when they are reminded of Hoppy.

No matter what their Hoppy represented, each was alive, robust, and active in their lives until they abandoned him. Then slowly, his image faded away, slipping a little more each day from the dream that had formed him—until one day they woke up and found their six-foot rabbit gone. He had left his tuxedo, hat, cane, and shoes on the floor next to their beds.

However, my brave quester Carol soon sees that no one else believes in Hoppy, so she stops trying to describe or defend her friendship with him—because she knows that at one time in their lives, they each abandoned their quests. She quickly becomes emotionally vulnerable to rejection as she lives with Hoppy until they part company. Having obtained her dream, she lets Hoppy move on to someone else with a dream.

Quest Refined by Defining Mission

Now that we have defined the *vision* in the guise of Hoppy, let's turn to the *mission* as the other integral part of a quest. The mission is the practical logistics of achieving a quest. I mentioned this principal earlier, but it is worth repeating here.

The foundation of a mission is the decision to mount a quest. Once this decision has been made, the first part of a mission is to search for the resources to accomplish the vision. The second part of the mission is the actual implementation of the plan.

Let's take an example of vision and mission from American history. Lewis and Clark didn't decide one day to jump in a canoe and paddle up the Missouri River or cross uncharted wilderness to the Columbia River and then to the Pacific Ocean. Their adventure was over eight thousand miles, which required a plan. The mission began in President Thomas Jefferson's heart—his vision—after the Louisiana Purchase in 1803. Once the budget of $2,500 was approved by congress, Jefferson recruited Lewis and Clark.

Lewis and Clark, as the captains of the adventure, then began recruiting and training forty men for the expedition. These two leaders didn't grab men off the street, go into pubs, or lurk in the dark corners of city streets for their men. Part of the plan was to identify talents for survival needed to successfully complete the trip. Therefore, Lewis and Clark chose men who were sharpshooters, frontiersmen, and men accustomed to hunger, thirst, and exhaustion but who continued their treks anyway. You might call them the Green Berets, Force Recon, Army Rangers, or Seals of today.

The mission officially began in May of 1804 and was completed in September of 1806. In like manner, as we have seen from

Want to Get the Most out of Life?

my quester, Carol made the decision to attend nursing school and immediately began funding her dream by personal sacrifices.

Here are some of the most negative statements I have frequently heard that discourage a quest: "How can you be sure you will finish your education? What if you run out of money? What if your child becomes sick?"

My answer to this series of undermining questions is to look at the source. These questions of doubt usually come from someone who never in their life reached for the golden ring on the merry-go-round. In truth, jealousy and envy fill the naysayers' hearts, not concern for the individual. The words of caution are about not wanting the quester to achieve what was abandoned by the critic. Now, I know issues addressed by these questions may arise, but the person on the quest will find solutions and make adjustments.

What if Lewis and Clark worried about these types of questions before they began? I can tell you as a parent that had one of these men been my son, these and many other questions would have crossed my mind. However, also as a parent, I would have wished my son Godspeed—which I did when my son joined the United States Marines Corps when he was just a baby of eighteen.

Had Lewis and Clark listened to questions like these, the Louisiana Purchase territory would not have been explored at that time. Their work would not be the pioneering foundation for exploration in the history of America. In like manner, if Carol had listened to questions like these, she never would have become a nurse or be able to follow the path thus established to become a nurse practitioner or doctor.

There is one final thought on the mission of a quest. Rarely does any endeavor worth effort go according to plan, but no quest can be fulfilled without a roadmap. Planning is essential. It gives a quest structure and direction, and provides a beginning and an end. Plans also prepare the quester to face the "what ifs." By dealing with these contingencies, the person develops skillsets to navigate life.

Quest for Freedom

Without a quest, a person drifts through life and, at some point, will look back at a half-century of years with little or nothing to show for the experience—except debt. The floundering human feels like he is sitting in a boat in the middle of the ocean without a rudder or sail. In such a predicament, he is tossed back and forth in the waves and storms of life without direction. He struggles to stay afloat and—without a paddle—can't row in any definite direction. Soon, staying afloat becomes a way of life that he passes down to his children and grandchildren. Included in the inheritance is the notion that extending oars and hoisting a sail is an affront to the family because they have accepted just staying afloat as a permanent way of life.

In order for you to hoist your sails and extend your oars, here is a summary of this chapter:

Quest Summary

A. Quest: A decision to embark on a life journey
B. Vision: A clear picture in one's mind of what is to be achieved
C. Mission: First, identify your resources, then implement the plan.

Seven Principles to Accomplish a Quest:

1. It's never too late in life to begin a quest.
2. First, identify and clarify your quest, then search for the resources to accomplish it.
3. Don't heed the voices of doubters and naysayers.
4. Don't focus on what can go wrong in your quest but on what will work.
5. Plans are not foolproof, but they offer direction in times of uncertainty or emergency.
6. Identify a beginning and end of each quest.
7. Each completed quest lays the foundation for a new quest.

One man with conviction will overwhelm
a hundred with only opinions.
WINSTON CHURCHILL

— 2 —

Family Opposition to Developing Self

Self Defined

From this point forward, I will be using the term *self* frequently. What do I mean by the term? Let's see what Isaiah has to say on the topic: "Yet you, O Lord, you are our Father. We are the clay, you are the potter; we are all the work of your hand" (Isa 64:8).

In this passage from the Old Testament, the prophet writes that God is the potter of each individual: "Before I formed you in the womb I knew you, before you were born I set you apart" (Jer 1:5a). As a potter designs and molds his clay vessel into its final form, so too does God fashion the self as his touch gives life to the human psyche. "Did not he who made me in the womb make them? Did not the same one form us both within our mothers?" (Job 31:15). In the same way that a potter's hands gently hold his new vessel with refined delicacy, so too should the self be held within each person with gentle attention. The self is the core inside each human being.

Since self is the core inside each human being, when I use the term I am *not* referring to the self's family of origin, ethnic group, gender, or sexual preference. Neither will my words have any bearing upon their political affiliation, marital status, or religious beliefs or lack thereof.

Want to Get the Most out of Life?

"Family Opposition to Developing Self" may seem like a strange title. In the following chapters, you will read some horrendous stories that will leave you breathless. In some cases, you will perhaps cry and ask how parents and other relatives could mistreat their own flesh and blood in the manners described. In my counseling experience, I have learned that families often pose the greatest opposition to a member who is seeking to better him- or herself.

There are three reasons why these stories are based on information I compiled from numerous clients. First, to protect privacy and confidentiality. Second, because of the similarity of how these same abuses occurred, with minor variations, in so many unrelated families. None of these young employees knew what the other was telling me, so they had no idea that their experiences were part of a pattern. Third, I am attempting to present what I heard and saw without judgment.

I will begin this chapter by describing what I witnessed in the faces of so many employees. During my twelve years at this facility, a significant number of clients who'd been abused came for counseling. Many would come into my office with a pressing problem, such as marriage issues, financial instability, children acting out, addictions, and a variety of other life problems. I'd sit patiently and listen. However, as they talked, their faces and body language presented an underlying problem that had nothing to do with the issues they described in our counseling sessions.

Most of the employees appreciated my frank and direct approach. But I believe that even those who didn't, benefited from the seeds that were planted during our time together.

At this point, I began to ask employees open-ended questions: "What do you want out of life? What are your dreams? Do you have a vision for your life?" Posing these and other questions allowed me to more precisely pierce beneath the presenting problems—which in turn gave me a glimpse into their underlying, darker self, and I was better able to understand the cause-and-effect property relating to their problems.

I want to affirm that the scenarios I describe only represented a fraction of the five thousand employees. Most of the other staff members were happy in their jobs and only experienced what I would call minor family problems.

Focusing on this group of employees, I believe there were multiple assaults on the self. I believe these assaults were diverse in nature and content. However, these assaults had one goal in mind—to subjugate the person's self and, in this suppression, to break the will, making the person believe that a quest in life was out of his or her reach.

Assault on the Self Explained

At very early ages, the employees in this group began to experience assaults on the self that were complete, absolute, and unconditional. What do I mean by an early age? Collectively, I'd say most were before the age of five, with some a little earlier and others later, depending on the harshness of the family environment.

Sometimes the person had an obvious congenital or developmental weakness. The self suffered a great indignity and humiliation when the weakness was mocked. Like chickens in a coop where the weak is constantly pecked by the strong, this weakness was exploited by stronger selves, ensuring that being bullied became a lifestyle.

With a pattern in place, you can imagine how this denigrating lifestyle obstructed, denied, and squelched what was supposed to be a developing, blossoming self. Remember that early in life, this person did not yet have a whole, complete self. But what could have been a budding, innocent, full self was taken prisoner before it had a chance to blossom, grow, and mature.

To think of this scenario conceptually, read Matt 13:3–4: "A farmer went out to sow his seed. As he was scattering the seed, some fell along the path, and the birds came and ate it up." In almost the same way, the stronger selves plucked the seed of self from the soil before it could take root and grow.

This demoralization left only a hollow, empty shell of self who had to quietly and privately recover from the daily assaults. The convalescence of the daily wounds to self was achieved in the shadows of secrecy. Little pieces of self that survived the relentless assaults were hidden and patched together in clandestine settings. Anytime an original idea, thought, or belief was voiced by the hurting self, it was immediately quashed because the ones exerting the pressure felt threatened. Hence, for the self, keeping original thoughts—especially if they were good thoughts—was paramount.

What was left of self was a hodgepodge patchwork collage of should haves and musts as dictated by the more powerful selves who ruled over their lives. These externally imposed rules of how self should think, feel, and believe were obeyed and mimicked primarily out of self-preservation rather than cooperation.

The Power of the Tongue in Perpetrating Assaults

> When we put bits into the mouths of horses to make them obey us, we can turn the whole animal. Or take ships as an example. Although they are so large and are driven by strong winds, they are steered by a very small rudder wherever the pilot wants to go. Likewise the tongue is a small part of the body, but it makes great boasts. Consider what a great forest is set on fire by a small spark. The tongue also is a fire, a world of evil among the parts of the body. It corrupts the whole person, sets the whole course of his life on fire, and is itself set on fire by hell.
>
> All kinds of animals, birds, reptiles and sea creatures are being tamed and have been tamed by man, but no man can tame the tongue. It is a restless evil, full of deadly poison.
>
> With the tongue we praise our Lord and Father, and with it we curse men, who have been made in God's likeness. Out of the same mouth come praise and cursing. My brothers, this should not be. Can both fresh water and salt water flow from the same spring? My brothers, can a fig tree bear olives, or a grapevine bear figs? Neither can a salt spring produce fresh water. (Jas 3:3–12)

Family Opposition to Developing Self

James the apostle states the catastrophic impact the tongue can have on everyone. However, in terms of this group of employees, its power was worse than catastrophic. The tongues of parents and other relatives stripped the hide off their souls. Their hearts were open and laid bare like criminals hanging on crosses, Roman-crucifixion style. Nails were cast deep into their spirits. Their wrists and ankles were nailed into the family crosses of criticism from which they hung while the air of self was sucked out of their lungs.

This metaphorical depiction is the best way I can describe what I observed in so many employees who were in emotional and spiritual survival mode when they came for counseling. The irony is that the tongue-lashes on the emotional backs of my clients were inflicted by their parents and other close relatives.

Here are two stories to illustrate how beautiful, young, healthy employees who should have been embracing life, but instead, they were, at best, seeking to escape life because of their families' punitive tongues.

Two Stories of Assaults

1. No Eye Contact

When Jose entered my office, his head was bowed as he focused on the ground around his feet. Instead of sitting in a chair near my desk, he chose one as far away from my desk as possible. Even seated, he still looked at his shoes.

I introduced myself and he replied without raising his head. If I hadn't shot my arm out like a rocket to shake his hand, I don't think he would have seen it to respond. However, his grasp was weak as though his hand had no bones. At this point, I should have guessed he was not accustomed to being treated with respect.

After a few minutes of small talk to lessen the tension in the air, I asked politely why he wouldn't look me in the eye. He replied he didn't look anyone in the face and hadn't most of his life. I asked why and he was hesitant to answer.

Want to Get the Most out of Life?

However, after coaching, he finally talked about his travails. His details were vague and measured as though I was a police interrogator and not a counselor.

His tone was low and muffled, almost a whisper. Periodically, it sounded like he was mumbling. His verbal communication indicated to me that he was fearful to speak no matter how well-intentioned his questioner. However, when he began to describe his past, I understood why his demeanor was that of a convict on death row.

Jose was the youngest of four children and was physically abused both at home and at school. Boys beat him up daily and mocked him. They insulted him verbally with such epitaphs as being stupid, ugly, and useless, saying he'd never amount to anything. Of course, with him not offering self-defense, he was branded a coward and other emasculating adjectives I won't print.

Every day when he returned home from school, he'd have black and blue marks on his face, a split lip, a bloody nose, or all three. No one defended him because his own brothers were just as violent and cruel to him.

Finally, he learned that his best defense was to have a downward-cast face and never communicate unless spoken too. His goal anywhere outside of his room at home was to be anonymous, obscure—a ghost, if you would—so that he was unseen or invisible. To be imperceptible was to achieve safety, emotionally and physically.

From the time he woke up in the morning until he went to bed at night, he refused to have direct eye contact with anyone—family, friend, or foe. He was a handsome young man, so I asked him if he had a girlfriend and he said yes. It seems she was the only person he would look straight in the eye. They had known each other since high school and she was his only friend. They were living together and had been since graduating from high school, and were planning to be married in the near future.

Family Opposition to Developing Self

I asked him how his lack of eye contact was accepted at work. I was fearful employees might have been equally as cruel as what he had experienced in childhood. He informed me his fellow workers treated him fairly—probably because he arrived at his cubical early in the morning and did his work without much contact with other people. And since his girlfriend worked near him in our company, he would spend lunch and breaks with her.

I made an interesting observation during our conversation. If I asked an uncomfortable question, he would turn his head from side to side while verbally responding. The motion seemed like a conditioned response.

After much encouragement, he did momentarily look up into my face one time. In that second where his gaze met mine, there was fear. Instantly, he lowered his head like a turtle withdrawing into its shell for safety.

I asked him why he had come to my office. He replied he wanted to learn about self-confidence. However, we were not able to proceed far because none of my suggestions were well received. For example: Building self-confidence through academic achievement by pursuing higher education. He doubted he had the ability. Work on walking with your head up and shoulders back, and look people in the eyes. You would have thought I'd recommended he speak to an audience of hundreds. He shook his head, and in that moment I realized over twenty years of his life had been devoted to looking at the ground and he could see no way of changing that habit. Additionally, I suggested he take advantage of further counseling outside our corporate setting to use his EAP benefits, but he was not enthusiastic about the idea. I never heard from him again.

2. Don't Touch Me!

I will never forget the first day Anita came to see me. She was a pretty African American young lady who greeted me verbally but with no handshake. Nor did she like sustained eye contact. Unlike Jose, her eyes were not focused on the floor. She would look at me briefly but then immediately turn her head away. Her eyes were constantly surveying the room, never maintaining eye contact.

During our session, I learned that at one time she'd been a little overweight, but had lost several pounds through weight lifting and related exercises. I complemented her on her dedication. She revealed she'd completed three years of college, majoring in biology. Although she'd been an A student, she had quit her academics abruptly and her reason for quitting was somewhat hazy.

Finally, she discussed the nitty-gritty. She'd been sexually abused from the age of ten through her mid-teens. Her father, uncles, brothers, and other family members had been the perpetrators. Anita had finally escaped the abuse by moving out of the home. Sad to say, her mother had chosen not to report the abuse to child protective services.

Anita was called a slut, a whore, and additional slanderous characterizations to her virtue all her life. The sexual abuse and verbal assaults on her moral repute had left her cautious, shy, and almost paranoid about being touched. She didn't want to hug, cuddle, hold hands, or become physically close to anyone. And yet, she had a long-distance relationship with her boyfriend in the military stationed in another state.

I asked her how she paradoxically did not like physical contact yet could have sex. I learned it took her a long time to trust before she allowed sexual intimacy. When she engaged in sex it was with extreme caution and on her terms. Over time in this long-distance relationship, she had her doubts about her partner's fidelity. I never did understand why she stayed in the relationship.

The reason she came for counseling was to learn how to be more open and less withdrawn. I didn't want to hazard a guess as to her definition of withdrawn, so I asked. She explained how she avoided eye contact, not just with men but

Family Opposition to Developing Self

with people in general. She distrusted everyone, giving them a wide berth.

I explained that what she needed was more than I could offer in an onsite EAP setting. I provided the information she needed to contact counselors in the community through her EAP program. We visited a few times and I learned her boyfriend was planning to move to our city.

To this day, I believe she didn't attend any counseling after our visits, and I believe her relationship probably was not successful. My statements are based on years of experience and not because I think she failed in any way. The level of abuse a woman has experienced as a child often distorts her perception of men. These women believe most men are abusive, and since they have no experience with kind, respectful men, they shy away from kindness like the plague. In fact, many of these women will break up with a man who offers kindness with no strings attached because they fear developing a deeper intimacy.

The Suffering Self

I wrestled with how to best describe the nature of what happens to the emerging self in such brutal family environs. I believe the levels of abuse can be measured on a continuum of severity. This statement initially sounds morbid, possibly macabre, as there is no accurate way to describe another person's pain. Nor can we gauge how one's pain is less or more than another's.

I decided the most accurate way to depict the cruelty to the embattled selves is to say they fall into two categories: *broken* or *fractured*, and *shattered*. I use two medical conditions of human bones receiving physical trauma to describe how similar this is to the damages done to the self through emotional, mental, and psychological abuse.

Want to Get the Most out of Life?

1. Broken, Fractured Selves:

    "The Lord builds up Jerusalem; he gathers the exiles of Israel. He heals the brokenhearted and binds up their wounds" (Ps 147:2–3).

    In this quotation, the word *brokenhearted* literally means "broken like a stick snapped in two pieces." We learn that God has the ability to take a human heart that is broken in two pieces and permanently heal the wound.

    I believe this spiritual healing is like a broken bone mended in the human body. For example, our son broke his femur at the age of four. After Kirk had been in a body cast for six weeks, the bone was fully restored. We saw an X-ray of the location of the trauma. The bone was thicker where the break had occurred. The doctor explained it was the body's way of insuring a break will never happen again at this location.

    People like Anita with similar abuses in their past live through trauma that is not reported to the authorities. This denial of their legal rights forces them to adapt the best way they can in order to survive. Victims such as these are either honor bound to family or are afraid to report their abuse out of fear of further abuse. The following are some examples.

    First, a story about how a family valued the secret bond of family honor above the safety of their children.

    A mother and father of a daughter and son who were both under the age of ten came for counseling because they were considering a divorce. During our second visit, I learned there was a family member in his early teens who had for years molested many of his cousins, mostly males. The molestation usually occurred during sleepovers and at family gatherings in homes.

    I asked what had been done about it. They said that nothing had been done. It appears this sexual abuse in the clan had been kept secret. It was one of those secrets that everyone knew about but no one discussed. Hiding my anger, I ask why no steps had been taken to report this extended

Family Opposition to Developing Self

abuse. Their reply was that they didn't want Ricky or his family to be in trouble with the law.

Fuming, I continued, "So, you are telling me that your family is willing to risk your children's mental and emotional health to protect one boy?" They both replied without reservation, "Yes." The answer was stated as though there was something wrong with my questioning the decision.

My next and last question was a simple "Why?" Their immediate reply was that they as a family did not want their reputation in the community tarnished. I was astounded, so I then concluded out loud, "You are telling me that your family's reputation is more important than the law and your children?" Again, without hesitation they answered yes.

Based on my experience as a counselor, I can make the assumption that Ricky was molested in his youth, and maybe the abuse was ongoing. His self was broken as a result. To some degree, I can hypothesize that the family members were broken too, because they condoned Ricky's behavior by not reporting or condemning it.

The second story involves a mother who valued her marriage more than her child.

Bradley, a high school senior with top grades, came with his mother for counseling. I had already met with the mother previously. The student had been expelled from school several times due to his insolent behavior. He'd been accepted into a top university in Texas on a scholarship, but his mother worried he might be expelled before completing his first semester. After one session I understood why. Bradley was an angry young man, but at the time, I could not understand why.

He came from an upper middle-class family and had been raised by his biological mother and stepfather. His mother wanted me to "fix him" at eighteen, when he had been defiant for many years. As we met over several sessions, I learned he had a great intellect, was a superb debater, and excelled in math. His Achilles' heel was his belligerent attitude and challenging of authority.

Want to Get the Most out of Life?

In my last session with his mother, I finally learned the reason why this young man from a Christian home was so angry. He'd been sexually molested by his stepfather when he was ten and when he reported the abuse, his stepfather received minimal legal punishment. The stepfather apologized to Bradley and the three of them continued to live under the same roof.

What surprised me was that when the molestation was made public, this young man's biological mother stayed with the stepfather. There'd been no talk of divorce or separation, but Bradley's anger had eight years to fester and bloom in his defiant behavior. I asked the mother point-blank why she did not divorce her husband. Her answer was that she loved him. Is it any wonder Bradley was angry when he had seen his mother choose his stepfather over his safety?

Ironically, the young man in my office said all was forgiven and he bore his stepfather no ill will. In fact, he stated several times that they were the best of friends and got along perfectly. Bradley did not return for additional sessions.

2. Shattered Selves:

The first example under this heading is about real shattered bones. Many years ago when we lived in Rhodesia, I volunteered in the Rhodesian army and served as a medic. I believe I was on my third bush assignment with a company of men in the middle of nowhere. While at camp late one afternoon, we received a radio message saying one of our patrols had been ambushed. Only one soldier, Michael, was injured, and that injury was severe. His left leg had been shattered by bullets from an AK rifle. Thank the Lord there was a senior medic in camp with me. We rode in the ambulance to the site of the ambush and administered first aid to Michael.

His femur was shattered into bits and pieces. Bone and blood were scattered everywhere. It looked like a ravenous wolf had bitten a chunk out of his leg. He was on death's door because of blood loss, pain, and shock.

Family Opposition to Developing Self

We were about an hour's drive away from the nearest hospital in the city of Bulawayo. During the day, the trip would have been dangerous, but at night, the chance of us getting ambushed too was a dire possibility. Our ambulance was escorted by two armored carrier vehicles, pickup trucks that had fifty-caliber machine guns mounted in the beds, surrounded by armor plating.

No matter how much these vehicles could have protected us, I was still scared, and prayed while ministering to Michael. I was fearful of hearing the ping, ping, ping of AK bullets or even worse, the swoosh of an RPG rocket—neither of which I heard. "The righteous cry out, and the Lord hears them; he delivers them out of all their troubles. The Lord is close to the brokenhearted and saves those who are crushed in spirit" (Ps 34:17–18).

We finally arrived in Bulawayo, where we left our wounded soldier at the hospital. The next morning I paid him a visit. Thanks to the experience of the senior medic and the skilled doctors who operated on him for many hours, Michael's life was saved.

His left leg was in a sling, bandaged from thigh to foot. He had metal plates and screws holding his leg together and several more surgeries in his future. The surgeon was hopeful his leg could be saved. After we visited a few minutes, I left the ward thinking about our adventure and how much we owed God. God had saved that young man. We may have put the effort into driving him to Bulawayo, but God was there. "Lord, the God who saves me, day and night I cry out before you. May my prayer come before you; turn your ear to my cry" (Ps 88:1–2).

I feel at times that some of the young people I counseled had experienced events that shattered their selves. And like Michael's leg, they were also susceptible to rot and decay from chronic emotional injury. These shattered selves gather all their personal resources from within, which are weak at best, to make something of themselves after their latest failure. However, within the shattered self, they know the effort is futile. They sabotage their endeavors by asking questions: How long will this job last? Six months, twelve, eighteen? How long will my relationship last? How long will I work and attend night classes at college?

The shattered self's handicap is that the self has been under such severe assault for so long that there is almost nothing left of the self to meet newly set challenges. It is within this context that I want to present two more stories of the suffering self.

The first time I met Pam, I was impressed with two traits—her beauty and her intellect. I learned she spoke three languages: Spanish, her first language, English, and French. She'd been raised in a Central American country and had a first-class education. Although she had a degree in secondary education, she had decided to leave the field. During our visit, she revealed she was clinically depressed. I had a hunch she was not telling me everything that troubled her.

Pam cried a little and I sensed she needed the safe haven of a counselor's office to let down her defenses. Her problem was that she had learned she was not cut out for call center work but was unsure of which direction to follow. I suggested she return to teaching, but she nixed the idea, as she did not want to teach again. I asked what else appealed to her and she was unsure, but regardless of her choice, she would need more education to prepare for it.

She continued to cry and couldn't seem to settle down enough to return to her desk. I suggested I call her husband to collect her. She agreed, and while we waited, I learned she had been molested by her father at a very early age. The sexual abuse had continued until her early twenties.

Pam and I met several more times. As in many sexual abuse cases, the predator, her father, was still exerting control over her emotionally. He was addicted to his need to dominate and she responded in her conditioned need to be subjugated. She could not let him go in her mind and heart.

Family Opposition to Developing Self

Pam was hypnotized by her father's voice like a rat drawn to the Pied Piper. She had been drilled like a professional football player on the practice field of life so that her response to his command was instinctual. Pam and her father still talked regularly. However, from the way she referred to him, her shattered self was split between a variety of unhealthy emotions and unnatural feelings toward him.

About six months passed and I heard no more from her. One day just after lunch, I received an urgent request to help an employee who was alarming other workers by her behavior. I hurried to the location to find Pam crying and very angry. To some degree, her behavior seemed paranoid, as though people around her meant her ill will. However, these co-workers were concerned because she talked about a bomb and wanting to hurt other people.

While I talked with Pam in an all-glass conference office, a manager called the police. In our discussion, she denied saying anything about a bomb or threatening others, but she voiced concerns that some of her fellow employees meant to tarnish her reputation. Eventually she calmed down but continued to sob, and much of her talking was nonsensical.

I again suggested her husband come get her and Pam agreed. However, the police officers arrived before her husband. They had to talk with her alone to determine if she was a danger to herself or others. One policeman entered the conference room with her while his partner collected information from the rest of us outside the room.

Within a few minutes, there were five management personnel gathered in the hall outside the transparent office with me, along with two other police officers who'd just arrived and two corporate security personnel.

The situation in the conference room quickly became volatile. The police officer tried to escort Pam out, but she refused to go quietly. He couldn't restrain her, as she was agitated and hostile. The other policeman hastily entered and they were able to restrain her, although she was kicking and screaming.

Want to Get the Most out of Life?

These police officers were truly professional, because in spite of her ferocity toward them, they did their best to treat her with dignity. However, when someone in her mental condition has to be restrained, there is something dehumanizing about the process. Pam caused her own embarrassment and public humiliation, not the officers. All our hearts were shattered by sadness and compassion. I knew it was not the young woman we all knew and loved who was out of control, but the sexually abused little girl inside her. Decades of sexual abuse by her biological father had caused heartache and pain within her fractured self which erupted like Mount Vesuvius.

The two security personnel and I followed behind the police officers as they took Pam through the building and out to one of their vehicles. She resisted all the way, kicking and screaming about her unjust treatment. However, she did not reach the height of her madness until she was placed in the back seat of the police car. She became like a tigress bouncing around in a cage, seeking to claw her way out, until fatigue overwhelmed her. It seemed as if what little sanity remained in her shattered self finally met its *coup de grâce*.

The last story under this heading is about Yolanda. When I first met her, she impressed me with her tall, slender frame. She looked like she should have been a runway model and not a call center worker. She had immigrated from Central America and had lived in the US since her early teens. Yolanda was single, which surprised me, as I figured some young man would have snapped her up years ago. She revealed there had been a few unsuccessful attempts to lasso her in with a promise of marriage, but she didn't trust men.

Yolanda visited several times to discuss her bouts of depression, which often occurred after she'd broken up with a man, usually due to his infidelity. Obviously, she had no problem gaining young men's attention, but she seemed to attract the unreliable sort. She was of the generation that hooked up almost immediately but didn't date beforehand.

Family Opposition to Developing Self

It has always seemed to me that if more young women dated with defined sexual boundaries set before the first date, I would have fewer clients! At this advanced stage of my life, I still do not understand the dynamics of hooking up. As an observation, it appears that hooking up is a false-positive excuse to sleep together without attachments or commitments. The truth is, this dysfunctional relationship practice is to men's advantage and women's disadvantage.

My major argument is, who is at risk for pregnancy? The justification of the excuses "we are just having fun," or "we're determining our compatibility" has dangerous long-term spiritual implications, rarely discussed by the couple—the chief implication being a high rate of depression in women of all ages. A percentage of those depressed women will also become suicidal because they feel betrayed for one or more of the following reasons.

First, they have been exploited. They have been used for their bodies alone. There is no other way to view hooking up.

Second, there is no discussion or promise of commitment. The best expression I have heard that describes this fact is "Why purchase a cow when the milk is free?"

Third, when one party discovers the other party has been unfaithful—usually the male—dissolving the relationship becomes toxic. The toxicity occurs because no matter how a woman deludes herself about her sexual freedom, her nature still continues to feel deceived. She has cheapened the gift only a woman has to offer—the sanctity of her womb. When her womb is no longer held in the highest regard, its devaluation crashes like the stock market in 1929.

Fourth, hooking up ignores the fact that the sexual act is a union of heart and soul. The joining of the flesh is secondary. In the self-delusion that sex is only about the physical, the couple view sex as a form of pleasure without the entanglement of commitment. This definition misrepresents what actually happens in the hearts of the two partners involved.

Want to Get the Most out of Life?

Two people cannot engage in the most intimate act and not feel a divine bond.

This relationship fact is why so many women do not trust men. God made the woman—Eve—to be the stable force in marriage. Eve is the adhesive and foundation, which is why when she ignores this fact about how God created her, she is peeling away the adhesive and she breaks into small pieces.

The hooking-up type of relationship arrangement has been as baffling to me as the term "friends with benefits," which I also protest for the same above-stated reasons. Anyway, although I digress, this is the type of relationship world in which Yolanda conducted her love life.

Her family was either wealthy or upper middle class. However, the family dynamics were a little hazy. She did have a strict father who was verbally critical and, at the minimum, emotionally abusive. Although what she reported did not support sexual abuse, I always privately believed she'd been abused.

Like many attractive young girls with physically and emotionally abusive fathers, Yolanda needed approval from men but didn't trust them. She wanted and needed masculine acceptance, but in her shattered self, all she knew was masculine disapproval. For a reason I couldn't understand, Yolanda believed she had nothing to offer in a relationship and that she was not beautiful. If she measured her self-esteem and worth on a scale of one to ten, she'd score herself a one. No amount of reasoning and appealing to how God had created her with beauty made any change in her self-acceptance. She was ugly in her mind, and that was the end of discussion.

Veering to another topic, I attempted to discuss why she seemed to choose young men who were not responsible or reliable. For example, the latest young man who was living with her was only employed two days a week. He slept all day and watched TV while she worked and paid his expenses.

I posed many questions: "Don't you think it's unusual that he doesn't own a car but feels entitled to use your car when he needs it?" "Doesn't it set off an alarm to your personal dignity when he uses your car to pick up his child when it's his turn to visit?" "When was the last time he looked for a job or offered to replace the gas he used in your car?"

She just looked at me and smiled. It was the same blank expression I once saw on a cow in the middle of the road late at night. Although I could have easily plowed right into the animal, it stood there chewing grass, oblivious to its dangerous surroundings.

I continued with my questions: "Does it bother you that he already has one child that you know of?" "Are you troubled when he borrows money from you to pay his child support?" "What about the idea you threw out that he might be using your car to take other women out on dates?"

Again, I got a blank stare with a half-engineered smile. Nothing I said seemed to penetrate her pride—if indeed, she had any pride remaining. But finally, after several minutes of us staring at each other in silence, I got an answer that fit her persona.

"He promised he would be faithful."

I discounted her reply because I don't think even she believed it. But it was her only defense. Then I stated, "You always hook up with men who are beneath you and not worthy of you."

Her response? "Well, at least under these circumstances I have control."

That was the last time I saw her. I'm writing her story twelve years later, so she must be in her early forties. Sad to say, she is probably with someone else who is exploiting her. Although we never discussed alcohol abuse, I knew it became an escape for her.

The potential I saw in Yolanda had nothing to do with her beauty. In spite of her shattered self, there was a charming, intelligent young woman trying to emerge from a tortured soul. And to this day, the same young woman is still trying to escape from within the hollow, shattered self.

Want to Get the Most out of Life?

Before continuing a discussion about the self, I need to describe the pattern of sexual predators in the families of the group of employees I'm focusing on. During the twelve years of my counseling, I found defined patterns. These predatory patterns gave me a model from which to infer sexual exploitation when interviewing new client employees on the first visit.

In the following paragraphs I am going to list the predators by identifying the most frequent and likely to prey on female children, to the least frequent and likely to prey on female children. I am not saying that this list of predators from most to least predatory is universal, national, or statewide. This compilation is limited to the area in which the two call centers were located.

Five Most Frequent Types of Sexual Predators
(The following profiles contain graphic details.)

- Cohabitant or Common-Law Husband:

    Due to the nature of hooking up, men and women sleep together soon after they start going out together. Most young women will not sleep with a man until the second or third visit. But if the young woman has not slept with the young man by the fifth formal visit, then the young man usually moves on to another woman. However, there is one anomaly. I discovered that many young women go to bed with a man on the first date because they are lonely, they have a strong libido, or they fear that if they don't, the man won't ask them out again. This third reason seems to be the most prevalent.

    I hesitate to call what transpires in the times they go out together dating, because dating is about learning more about a potential partner to determine compatibility. However, what I have heard from young women is that when time is not spent in courtship but goes immediately to sexual behavior, the relationship becomes conflicted. First, physical attraction and sexual intimacy become confused with what they think is love. Then when the novelty of the physical act diminishes,

Family Opposition to Developing Self

the couple assume they don't love each other anymore. This is followed by one of the partners breaking up. It is usually the young man who terminates the unhealthy relationship because he has secretly partnered with someone new who is more sexually active with him.

I give this brief background about coupling because oftentimes the young lady in question may have a daughter or two. The fact that these children see mom sleeping with a new man communicates in their minds that he is also a new daddy. Over time, Mom might not insist on modest clothing and may become lax with the daughter. In addition to a decline in modesty, the daughter will jump into bed with Mom and "Dad."

This breakdown in boudoir boundaries is gradual, creating an artificial sense of family. The next step for the young man is to exploit the new family circumstances by going into the young girl's bedroom at night while her mother is sleeping—ostensibly to say goodnight or to see if the girl is all right. Any unnatural act, from touching to sexual intercourse, will occur. The daughter is slowly groomed to accept Daddy's hands in private places until she accepts the act as normal. Then the girl is maneuvered into believing Daddy's sexual desires are normal. However, the young girl is confused and afraid, so a report will not be given to the mother.

- Legal Stepfather:

    The legal stepfather is the second most frequent offender. What I explained about the predatory practices of common-law husbands or cohabitants equally applies to the legal stepfather. However, he may have easier access because he is actually married to the mom. Some of the ways this predator grooms the daughter to accept inappropriate touching is by playing games such as wrestling or tickling. In time and with regular practice, when he deliberately touches the girl, she accepts the action as almost normal and is less uncomfortable.

    There will be an internal confusion in the girl's heart. Nature tells her in her budding femininity that where he is placing his hands is wrong. Yet, because touching inappropriately has happened so often, she will tell herself it's all right, he is her dad. And Dad wouldn't do anything wrong.

The stepfather might also have the girl sit on his knee and ride the horsey as his leg goes up and down and around with the child straddling his knee and thigh. This riding the horsey may eventually lead to the girl sitting directly on his lap over his genitals, which have by this time become aroused. I'll leave the rest of the predatory behavior to the readers' imagination. He will continue to break further appropriate boudoir etiquette, thereby lowering the boundaries of respecting the girl's emerging womanhood.

Some of these young girls might find that the touching feels good, but they know instinctively that is it inappropriate. They end up riddled with guilt and self-blame, which will prevent them from telling anyone, let alone their mothers.

- Biological and Step-Grandfathers:

    Grandfathers are the third most frequent group of predators. Their predatory behavior is the same as the first two groups, but they have easier access to the girls. Since many grandparents take care of their grandchildren overnight for a number of reasons, this makes the granddaughters particularly vulnerable.

    During a sleepover, the grandfather will sneak into the granddaughter's room at night. He will either remove the sheet and blankets, slip his hands under the covering, or lay in bed with the child until his sexual needs are met.

    I have learned that when grandmothers turn a blind eye, it is usually because the idea of the abuse of their grandchildren is too horrendous for them to digest. It is easier to ignore if they can pretend it didn't happen. Usually in these cases, the grandfather also molested his daughter as well.

    Then there are the stories of the sweet old grandfather who engages in kisses and hugs. You may wonder what's

Family Opposition to Developing Self

wrong with kissing and hugging. All he wants is to be close to his precious grandchildren by being affectionate.

Over the years, I heard numerous reports about grandfathers whose kisses on the lips included extensive use of the tongue. This same type of clandestine, sexual kissing is equally pursued by the first two categories of sexual offenders I wrote about in previous paragraphs.

Often the girl is so surprised by this type of kissing that she becomes uncomfortable and will in the future avoid greeting and kissing her grandfather. But that is not the end. The girl's mother might not be aware of the inappropriate kissing, and will insist that her daughter kiss her grandfather and not be disrespectful.

However, sad to say, there are times when the mother is aware of this inappropriate kissing because she was molested in the same way by her father. He was never challenged by family or the law for sexually violating his daughter—the girl's mother—and now he has open *carte blanche* to the granddaughter.

- Biological and Stepbrothers:

    The fourth category of sexual offenders is not usually so insidious. What normally happens is that when fueled by hormones, natural curiosity overrules common sense. Why brother and sister are different is finally explored. I believe that if there is touching, viewing, or both, it is because of inquisitiveness. And usually after a few times of crossing intimacy boundaries, the behavior stops.

    Those children involved usually feel guilty because of the observation and touching, but the behaviors cease before they get out of control. However, if the kids derive pleasure from the activity, they might continue these improprieties. Instinctively and from parental teaching, they know what they are doing is morally wrong.

    Now, in cases where daughters are abused by their significantly older brothers, or brothers are sexually abused by significantly older sisters, the methods are much in the same manner as I have previously written.

The older brother is typically in his mid-teens and his sister is usually around ten or eleven, when her womanhood is starting to bloom. Yet this is not a hard and fast rule, because some brothers have molested sisters much younger than what I have just described, which is also true when the sexual roles are reversed.

This older male teen predator's incestuous sexual appetite is fueled by raging hormones, pornography, and opportunity. He will force himself on his sister because she is afraid to say no. This practice can become as regular as a few times a week or whenever opportunity presents itself. Usually, the only way it stops is when the younger sister grows older and stronger so she can physically fight him off. In other cases, the older brother leaves the home to work or attend college. Sadly, in other cases, the sexual abuse continues until the girl leaves home in her late teens for college or work.

This abuse is kept a secret because the girl is ashamed and embarrassed and feels she has no control over her body. She can also be threatened with bodily harm by the older brother. In many cases, when a girl has told her mother, the mother doesn't believe her. The daughter is then punished for lying about such a terrible accusation.

- Uncles or Cousins:

    Uncles and cousins are pretty much opportunists, so they don't have the same frequency of molesting their nieces or nephews as the other groups of predators. However, a good way to tell if they are molesting relatives is watching a daughter's reaction when she is told uncles and cousins are coming over for a family visit—or alternatively, when the daughter is told her family is going to the uncle's or cousin's house. In either option, observation will show that the daughter will avoid being near the uncle or cousin.

    If she practices avoidance, there's a good chance something may be happening when the daughter is alone with

Family Opposition to Developing Self

the uncle or cousin. Parents need to question the daughter privately at home so that confidentiality can shield her from retribution. I would also suggest that parents question their daughter even if no aberrant behavior is suspected. Never assume that your child, girl or boy, is safe in the homes of friends or relatives. You may live to regret it.

Here Is an Instance of the Abuses I Just Related

If I had to write a title to Janet's story, it would be "All I Want Is a Hug, Please." When I met her, she was in her thirties. She had dishwater blond hair and was ordinary in appearance by today's standards, dressed in plain clothes which neither highlighted nor accentuated her femininity. Her demeanor struck me as being lost. She did have one goal—to become a paralegal. Beyond stating that goal, she appeared to be socially helpless.

Janet was married to a convicted sexual offender whom she believed had reformed. However, as she and I learned over time, he had not changed his behavior. She reported that he seldom worked a steady job and his personal habits and hygiene were unhealthy.

During this first session, she revealed that for most of her life before she left home, many of the males in her family had sexually molested her repeatedly. She'd never experienced being hugged by a father, or any man for that matter, without sexual overtures.

At the end of the first session, I asked if she would like a hug. To preface this action, I need to tell you that I have two adult children, both at least a decade older than Janet, and I wanted to treat her as if she were my child. We embraced for about thirty or forty seconds. I thought that was long enough and attempted to let go. But she clung to me like a child who felt she was about to permanently say goodbye to her daddy. I continued to hold her as if she were my forty-two-year-old daughter.

Janet finally let go, and when she left my office, she had a little spring to her step. During our second meeting the next week, she requested if we could begin with a hug and I agreed. And at the end of the session we hugged again.

Want to Get the Most out of Life?

What I concluded was that although she was a young woman, there was an abandoned girl-child inside her, orphaned by horrible sexual abuse by the very males in her life who should have been her protectors. She knew sexual touch but she didn't know a fatherly embrace. For the first time in her life, she was discovering the natural touch of a father in an appropriate way.

From the third session on, we began and ended each session with a fatherly embrace. When I forgot to hug her, she always reminded me. I have had cases like this before with both young women and men, but there was something unusual about Janet.

My impression was that at some point in her young life she had stopped allowing herself to feel sexual emotions out of self-preservation of her mental and emotional health. I think it became too painful for her to expect appropriate affection from males only to be repeatedly disappointed by sexual overtures. To illustrate, think of being in a windowless room and switching off the light. You are left in pitch darkness. So Janet switched off her emotions and lived in the darkness devoid of emotion.

During our last session, we discussed her present situation and her future plans. Now that she was divorced, she could pursue the education she needed to meet her professional goals. I reminded her that she had to avoid relationships that would deter her from pursuing her quest to fulfil her purpose.

All the sad, sensational stories I shared in this chapter illustrate what occurs in some elements of society. If you find yourself in a similar situation, get help and remove yourself from the toxic environment. Developing your complete self is of prime importance.

Therefore we do not lose heart. Though outwardly we are wasting away, yet inwardly we are being renewed day by day. For our light and momentary troubles are achieving for us an eternal glory that far outweighs them all. So, we fix our eye not on what is seen, but on what is unseen. For what is seen is temporary, but what is unseen is eternal.

2 CORINTHIANS 4:16–18

— 3 —

The Role of Pastoral Employee Counseling

A Bible On My Desk

When I was blessed to start my job with this company in November 2007, I made a personal commitment. I determined I would not counsel any differently in this corporate world than I would in a Christian setting. What then is the difference between pastoral and corporate counseling? Pastoral counseling focuses on spiritual and familial dynamics, whereas corporate counseling focuses on psychological and social dynamics as well as human growth and development.

I brought my Bible to work on the first day and laid it on my desk—not in a prominent place but along with other reference books. My Bible is light blue and the words *Holy Bible* are centered in gold at the top, and my name is at the bottom on the right.

I also developed personal ground rules about how I would use my Bible:

- I wouldn't draw attention to it.
- I would never state I was a Christian or ask if the client was a Christian.
- I would never ask if an employee would like me to read from the Bible.

- I would never ask if an employee wanted us to pray together.
- No matter the faith of the employee, I would treat them all the same.

You may be thinking, Why did you do everything you could to avoid mentioning the Bible and your Christian faith?

My answer is that God does not need our help to spread his Word. And I learned that when we try to help the Lord, we get in his way.

Here is my simple explanation of how my role changed and developed.

First Phase of Greeting Employees for Counseling

The first time an employee came to see me, I would always begin in the same way. I identified who I was, told them my role on the campus, and explained what to expect in counseling. At the end of our two-session assessment, I would refer the employee to an EAP counselor in the community who was contracted as a vendor.

Then the Holy Spirit began to take charge. One day an employee came in and asked if I was a Christian counselor. I answered in the affirmative, but added that I was there for everyone no matter their faith.

I was later asked if I counseled any differently onsite than I did at my church, where I was also a contract counselor. My answer was negative, but I said I would in no way place pressure on employees to accept my faith. However, they needed to know I used a biblical approach to deal with all issues. When I was asked the rational for my belief, I informed the employee that after twenty-five years of counseling, I had found that the Bible had the best answers to man's problems.

The answer from the employee was, "Fair enough."

Another time an employee came to see me and said, "I hear you are a Christian counselor." Again I answered yes, but said I would never pressure anyone to change his or her beliefs. Guess

The Role of Pastoral Employee Counseling

what the client said to me? "Great. I feel better with a Christian counselor." And then she sat down and we began to talk.

"The Lord is my light and my salvation—whom shall I fear? The Lord is the stronghold of my life—of whom shall I be afraid?" (Ps 27:1).

On several occasions I had employees walk into my office, notice the Bible on my desk, and—before I could utter a word—say, "I'm glad you are a Christian. My anxiety level dropped the moment I saw your Bible."

"Cast all your anxiety on him because he cares for you" (1 Pet 5:7).

Before I begin phase two of how the Holy Spirit was working in my job, you need to know that the events I just described took place probably over a year or more. During that time, people who came to visit me returned to their work stations and reported my approach to their fellow employees. My referrals started increasing purely by word of mouth—an odd occurrence in our secular, humanist world. Yes, I attended large and small corporate meetings and marketed myself as their new counselor, but something greater was happening. But at the time I was too spiritually blind to be aware of it. It was only upon reflection that I realized how powerful God's Word is when other people think it's dormant. Sometimes it is best if we take ourselves out of the equation and let God work in his way and in his time.

Second Phase of Greeting Employees for Counseling

Truthfully, I cannot remember what happened first. Either the Holy Spirit talked to my heart and I asked an employee if he wanted me to read a Bible passage that applied to his problem, or an employee asked me to read a passage that applied to his problem. Either way, a floodgate opened—or you might say the Red Sea was parted, with God leading the way.

I changed my initial standardized greeting to new employees who came to see me. I now included a comment about the Bible. I would read and apply the Scriptures but only if the employee made such a request. Like a lawyer in a courtroom, I got the employee to verbally agree or refuse. Very few employees refused, and of course I respected their decision.

After I began this new approach of reading Scripture, I noticed time and again the positive effects on the clients. Light seemed to glow in their faces and new hope glistened in their eyes. I witnessed tears turn into laughter. Joyous attitude instead of depression. Some clients came into my office suicidal but left comforted, rejoicing, and able to cope better with life. This change in disposition was because of God's Word.

"For I am the Lord, your God, who takes hold of your right hand and says to you, 'Do not fear; I will help you'" (Isa 41:13).

I need to make several observations about this approach to counseling.

First: As a secularly trained counselor I never witnessed traditional therapy have the same transforming impact on people's hearts. Traditional secular therapy may have touched their minds, but never their hearts.

Second: What I saw in the privacy of my office was not science, but the power of God's Word.

Third: As an employee's spirit was uplifted, so too was his mind cleansed from the debris of unhealthy thoughts.

Fourth: This miracle continued for the remainder of the years I was employed. There were many times I wanted to go home at night and share with my wife:

"God's Word ministered to a severely battered and bruised wife."

"God's Word helped a pregnant girl whose boyfriend abandoned her."

"God's Word comforted a mother whose baby accidently strangled himself to death while trying to climb out of his crib."

"God's Word strengthened a mother who has three children and a drug-addicted husband who regularly spends all their money on cocaine."

"God's Word gave solace to a woman who bellowed in my office for over two hours. His Word gave her courage to finally face her broken heart. She had suffered severe battering over the twenty years of her marriage. She had always felt it was her duty to keep it secret but today she opened up!"

"God's Word helped another woman cry as though she were on death row. She needed to vent because she was afraid to return home. Her husband is so abusive she lives in terror every day for her life."

However, because I am a counselor bound by confidentiality, I cannot name specific clients, nor can I use information that would allow a reader to identify them. I have to place all this pain in my employee's lives in a uniquely sealed box and sequester it in a subconscious warehouse that officially doesn't exist. All counselors learn how to insulate, store, and act as though what they hear has no adverse effects on their hearts. They each have their own method of absorbing, digesting, and overcoming what they hear.

Fifth: Since I cannot divulge specific information, millions of angels in heaven rejoice as they witness the power of God's Word change the lives of my clients.

Sixth: It is comforting to read a beautiful passage of Scripture and receive chills lasting seconds. But it's exhilarating to see God's Word sail like a javelin straight into the heart of darkness in person after person. The following passage spoke to my faith in a different way after witnessing the impact of the javelin of truth.

"For the word of God is living and active. Sharper than any double-edged sword, it penetrates even to dividing soul and spirit, joints and marrow; it judges the thoughts and attitudes of the heart. Nothing in all creation is hidden from God's sight. Everything is uncovered and laid bare before the eyes of him to whom we must give an account" (Heb 4:12, 13).

Seventh: I also reflected on what the apostle Peter wrote to the churches of Pontus, Galatia, Cappadocia, Asia, and Bithynia in the first century.

"But in your hearts set apart Christ as Lord. Always be prepared to give an answer to everyone who asks you to give the reason for the hope that you have. But do this with gentleness and respect, keeping a clear conscience" (1 Pet 3:15–16).

Gentleness is the key. Every employee who came for counseling needed the tenderness of God's Word. There is something calming about the kindness of God's Word when offered like a cup of refreshing cold water to moisten the dry tongue of anguish.

Eighth: Paul wrote in his second letter to Timothy a passage that further highlights the solemn yet nurturing nature of God's words.

"All Scripture is God-breathed and is useful for teaching, rebuking, correcting and training in righteousness, so that the man of God may be thoroughly equipped for every good work" (2 Tim 3:16–17).

Here we have the confidence that God's Word is plainly *breathed* by him. When God speaks, his words are holy and righteous because they come from him. And what he speaks is pure and perfect because he is pure and perfect. One biblical commentator I read stated that when we puff on a window in icy-cold weather, the vapor trail of our breath is metaphorically similar to what God did with the Bible.[1] He breathed words through the hands of the biblical writers.

Third Phase of Greeting Employees for Counseling

Several years passed and one day an employee I'd not met previously came for a visit. Beth's distressing revelation of trauma was one of the worst cases I had heard. Frankly, one of the many lessons I learned while at the facility was how much abuse women can suffer and still survive. I would often advise individuals and groups on campus to be kind to fellow employees. You do not know the trials and tribulations some of them are enduring in their marriages. Nor do you know of the abysmal life some of them had growing up.

Here I would like to offer some supporting statistics about the female employees I encountered during my twelve years. I estimate that four out of ten women had a history of sexual abuse

---

1. Source unknown.

which usually began before the age of ten. I would also comfortably say that about 30 percent of the women were in an abusive relationship. Finally, I would suggest that about 30 percent of the women who were married or cohabitating were with men who:

- refused to work
- only worked when it suited them
- came and went from the home at will and were gone for weeks or months at a time
- used the family income to support their alcohol or drug addiction
- were abusive to the wives and children
- probably sexually abused the girls primarily, and sometimes the boys
- had one or more mistresses

These are some of the issues many of the women who came for counseling faced, and the reason why I asked Beth if she would like to pray. There was no hesitation in her voice as she immediately agreed. Instinctively and without thinking, I asked if she was a hand-holder and when she nodded, I held out my hand to her. Together as fellow Christians, we approached the Lord's throne in prayer, hand in hand.

Opening a session with a prayer added a new dimension to how I greeted new clients. Also, you need to know that this change gradually evolved over several years and then became standard practice.

Now when employees came to see me, I openly informed them that I was a Christian, that I believed the Bible had the answers to all of life's problems, and that I would only use the Bible if they wanted me to and would respect their right to refuse. Again, very few employees refused. I also informed them I believed in prayer and would pray with them only if they wanted to pray. I began telling employees, male and female alike, that I was a hand-holder, but assured them I would not pray with them or hold hands if they felt uncomfortable.

Real Men Do Pray and Hug, Sometimes Both at the Same Time!

When I added the praying-together component to my sessions, I found about 70 percent of the men I asked agreed to pray and only about 50 percent of those men wanted to pray holding hands. I need to say here that holding hands with men was a powerful experience. For some of the younger ones, it was like father and son. My instincts also told me these younger men either had never prayed with their fathers or if they had, they had never held their fathers' hands in prayer.

The older ones really loved having a big brute of a guy like me with whom to pray. They knew I'd been in the military, played football, and had several overseas counseling jobs in places like Casablanca and Kabul, Afghanistan. I don't think they had much of a chance to pray with another man as intimately as we did in my office. I know our intimacy in prayer touched a part of their souls previously not embraced.

Some of the men with whom I prayed became more open in public greetings. We no longer shook hands but embraced like brothers in Christ. However, with some men it was also like an embrace with a fellow warrior who had been in combat. With others, it was like guys who had both played high school football..

One of these clients was a young male who was built like a Sherman tank from World War II. I believe his neck was as thick as my thigh. He was a former Marine and an expert in the martial arts. Yet he was as soft as a marshmallow inside. He was like a big teddy bear. But don't cross him or you would be on the ground, writhing in pain.

We had a special intimacy which I cherish to this day because at its heart was Jesus. When we met anywhere, we always hugged like two big bears and squeezed until neither of us could hold any longer. When we prayed in the privacy of my office, we held hands facing each other like two football players squatting on a football field. However, we were both too old and our knees were too worn out, so we sat in chairs. We prayed for his marriage and we prayed for his children and we prayed for his new life in Jesus Christ.

"Greet one another with a holy kiss. All the churches of Christ send greetings" (Rom 16:16).

Here are a few more verses on what a powerful tool prayer can be in a Christian's life.

"If we confess our sins, he is faithful and just and will forgive us our sins and purify us from all unrighteousness" (1 John 1:9).

"Therefore confess your sins to each other and pray for each other so that you may be healed. The prayer of a righteous man is powerful and effective" (Jas 5:16).

"Do not be anxious about anything, but in everything, by prayer and petition, with thanksgiving, present your requests to God. And the peace of God, which transcends all understanding, will guard your hearts and your minds in Christ Jesus" (Phil 4:6, 7).

"The Lord is near to all who call on him, to all who call on him in truth" (Ps 145:18).

What About the Unbeliever?

The company I worked for has a global presence, so there were employees from many non-Christian faiths, such as Hinduism and Islam. I had some interesting conversations with employees who followed these faiths. Usually at the beginning of a session, I would express my regret that I did not have an intimate knowledge of their religion and would ask them to please forgive me if I said something offensive. This seemed to set the tone of our conversations. However, I also learned they were westernized, so they were flexible when dealing with people of other faiths. Even though I didn't know much about their belief systems, it seemed they were not easily offended.

Although I never met any, I am sure many other non-Christian religions were represented in such a large employee base. We might have even had a few witches or warlocks. I knew of one coven in another corporation of the city.

Seriously, I sought to follow the apostle Paul's example from two thousand years ago when he was in the Areopagus in Athens.

"Men of Athens! I see that in every way you are very religious. For as I walked around and observed your objects of worship, I even found an alter with this inscription: TO AN UNKNOWN GOD. Now what you worship as something unknown I am going to proclaim to you" (Acts 17:22–23).

I never sought to convert employees who did not believe in Jesus, but chose to be their friend. Like Paul, if I was asked, I would do my best to tell them about Jesus in as humble and respectful a manner as possible. I tried to be "all things to all men" (1 Cor 9:22).

Before I leave these three phases of becoming a Christian counselor in a secular company, I think it's important to know from where I drew my inspiration for my methodology. I got it from the apostle Paul:

> Though I am free and belong to no man, I make myself a slave to everyone, to win as many as possible. To the Jews I became like a Jew, to win the Jews. To those under the law I became like one under the law (though I myself am not under the law), so as to win those under the law. To those not having the law I became like one not having the law (though I am not free from God's law but am under Christ's law), so as to win those not having the law. To the weak I became weak, to win the weak. I have become all things to all men so that by all possible means I might save some. I do all this for the sake of the gospel, that I may share in its blessing. (1 Cor 9:19–23)

Pastoral EAP Counseling

In about the sixth year in the trenches dealing with clients who had past emotional baggage and severe domestic issues, I began to feel a change in my role. Those employees became my *family*. I no longer felt like a corporate EAP onsite counselor. In my heart, I felt

The Role of Pastoral Employee Counseling

like a *pastoral* EAP counselor. The problem with this new role was that there is no such designation. A person in my position can either be a pastoral counselor or a corporate EAP counselor, but not both. Or so I thought. But I loved my five thousand employees—not to say that other EAP counselors didn't love their corporate charges or that I was the first one to feel this way.

On a daily basis, when I came to work and saw employees I'd counseled, it was natural to ask about their families. How's your son who just passed his CPA exam? Has your situation improved since you have moved away from your abusive paramour? Now that you have finished your BS in psychology, when are you starting your master's?

In more ways than one, I felt like the pastoral counselor of a large suburban church one day and a corporate EAP counselor the next. It seemed natural that the two finally became one, at least in spirit. At the same time this was happening, I was able to formulate an answer to my question: Why do so many of these young people have no vision for their future, purpose for their lives, or quest to pursue? And the best way to describe it is by using two passages from the same story in the New Testament.

The Lesson of the Empty House

"When an evil spirit comes out of a man, it goes through arid places seeking rest and does not find it. Then it says, 'I will return to the house I left.' When it arrives, it finds the house unoccupied, swept clean and put in order. Then it goes and takes with it seven other spirits more wicked than itself, and they go in and live there. And the final condition of that man is worse than the first. That is how it will be with this wicked generation" (Matt 12:43–45). The parable is repeated in Luke 11:24–26.

In this parable, Jesus refers to the soul as a house. It's a metaphor indicating that the soul has a dimension, size, and space. Perhaps not as we mortals understand, but in the spiritual world, our souls can house a multitude of demons and their lieutenants. The soul and its parts will house something—if not of God, then of Satan. There's another danger the parable offers as an additional lesson. Although the soul may be swept clean and thereby pass the white-glove inspection, if it's not immediately offered to God as its new occupant, then the original demon and his compatriots can reenter.

I would like to follow some logic in this metaphor of the house for the soul. I believe using this two-thousand-year-old metaphor will make better sense when compared to a twenty-first-century new home.

In our American culture, young families begin their housing investments by purchasing starter homes. Usually they are small or need renovations to improve the quantity and quality of the functioning living space. Once the couple moves into their new starter home, they begin to have children, or if they already have one child, they will give birth to more. Then the prosperous couple begins earnestly searching for another, larger home or makes constructional improvements to their first home.

I have known young couples who purchased starter homes that required a great deal of effort by the husband. He worked at night during the week after business hours and all day Saturday and Sunday to add improvements. All the couple's efforts, thoughts, and dreams were geared to one goal—a new, improved home from an old home.

It occurred to me in reading this parable that there's a reflective assessment necessary for its application to mortal spirituality. In the parable, the demon returned to his original house and discovered it empty. He also discovered it well cared for and clean. Therefore, he brought seven more demons with him. Now the hapless human has eight demons in the home occupying his soul. Could this not be a parable with a second meaning?

Look at how much energy and treasure people expend in searching for and acquiring homes for their families on earth. Why? Because they love their spouses and children and want to protect them from the elements. They don't want the wind, storms, and rains, along with the blazing hot sun, to harm them. Could we not equally apply this determination in the spiritual realm?

The Role of Pastoral Employee Counseling

It would seem prudent for humans to construct a solid foundation, walls, and sturdy roof for their families' hearts and souls, too. There are not only life storms, fluctuating winds, and drenching rains challenging their faith, but there are demons as well. Give a demon half a chance and he will spin a lie seemingly so true that his misdirection will steal the soul of the most unsuspecting Christian. In conclusion, we need to keep our house clean, but full of the Holy Spirit.

"Be self-controlled and alert. Your enemy the devil prowls around like a roaring lion looking for someone to devour. Resist him, standing firm in the faith, because you know that your brothers throughout the world are undergoing the same kind of sufferings" (1 Pet 5:8–9).

The apostle Paul provided us a warning: "For such men are false apostles, deceitful workmen, masquerading as apostles of Christ. And no wonder, for Satan himself masquerades as an angel of light. It is not surprising, then, if his servants masquerade as servants of righteousness. Their end will be what their actions deserve" (2 Cor 11:13–15).

Demons and their lieutenants don't care how clean or dirty a house may be if it's empty. They will move in, and like a bunch of frat boys in a frat house in college, the more the merrier. And once they move in, it's extremely difficult to terminate their lease! Have you tried expelling a frat boy from his room?

On a personal note, my wife and I owned a small house several decades ago which cured me of wanting to go into the real estate business. We had renters in it for several months who didn't pay their rent, and by law we could not force them to move. By the time they left—in the dark of the night, I might add—the inside of the house appeared as though someone had used a wrecking ball. There were holes in the walls, a window air-conditioning unit had been destroyed, the carpets smelled, and the list went on.

I believe a case like our disappointing experience with renters is a great example of what happens with humans who allow demons to reenter their homes. Before our renters moved in, we made sure all the appliances worked and were clean. However, like in this parable, once demons move in and throw their wild parties, no one can estimate the amount and the cost of damage that can be done to the human soul.

During my twelve years as an onsite EAP counselor, I made a profound observation. Despite the secular humanist society in which we live, in private these young people all stated they knew there was life after death. Most of them had been raised Catholic and many were Protestants. But regardless of their faith—whether they stated it or not—they felt guilty because in their minds they had abandoned their church.

They didn't have to tell me this because I could see it on their faces. No matter how rudimentary a person's faith, in the throes of tragedy, heartbreak, or loss, there is something in the human spirit that reaches for God. The intangible, hidden seed in every soul will not abandon the one who formed it. Mortals do not understand him nor can they control him, but in crisis, mortals always search for him because their spirits tell them he exists.

Yes, there were some people who attended church every Sunday, but during the rest of the week their lives were a far cry from the holiness they practiced on Sunday. I noticed their confusion and frustration in their voices and on their faces. They knew there had to be something more than ritualistically attending a church service. Their problem was that like most of us, they had been taught all their lives that Christianity is a ritual. As long as the ritual was followed, then that was all Christ asked for. No wonder they had a faith as empty and shallow and dry as an oasis scorched by the sun. They didn't know any better.

"How long must I wrestle with my thoughts and every day have sorrow in my heart?" (Ps 13:2).

"I am worn out from groaning; all night long I flood my bed with weeping and drench my couch with tears. My eyes grow weak with sorrow; they fail because of all my foes. Away from me, all you who do evil, for the Lord has heard my weeping. The Lord has heard my cry for mercy; the Lord accepts my prayer" (Ps 6:6–9).

Yes, I believe God hears our cries for mercy and wants to help. In the next chapter, I will propose that if we want to have purpose on this earth, we must first have purpose in God. If we want to pursue a quest for freedom on this earth, we must first seek a quest for freedom from sin. And finally, there is not a soul God has created that is without a purpose. He wants us to have purpose so we won't be in bondage to sin. He also wants us to be free in Jesus by his blood on the cross, as that is the only way to be truly free.

A Refuge, Demons Stilled, and Peace

The next two stories are examples that reveal the heartaches and pain some of my clients struggled with. Many employees revealed that the hour or two we spent together with the door closed was like a sanctuary for them. It was a time when their demons were stilled and they had refuge and peace.

1. A Safe Word (The following story contains graphic details.):

    A timid mouse of a young lady came for counseling. Stephanie was what other people would call a plain Jane. However, if she had accentuated her God-given femininity, she could have discovered her inner and outer beauty.

    Within seconds of her opening-up, I privately presumed she had a shattered self. Like so many young women I had seen, she'd had a childhood of physical and sexual abuse and emotional neglect. Yet in her case, its nasty residue led to a life of sadomasochism. Stephanie came to see me because she was concerned about her love life. She was engaging in three-way sex with two men who were in love with her. One was a little closer in age to her and the other was nearly old enough to be her father.

    During our discussion, she revealed she was struggling morally with the idea of three-way sex with two men who wanted to marry her. They both knew they were in competition for her affection as rivals. And her dilemma was that if she continued in this arrangement, she would be unfaithful no matter what she did. We discussed the situation in depth and this is when she revealed she was into sadomasochism.

She also disclosed that she had engaged in this practice with each suiter individually, although she didn't go into graphic detail. She left my office feeling a little better because she had aired all her reasons for and against a permanent relationship with either man.

I didn't see her again for about nine months. During that time, she had made her decision and chose to marry the man nearly old enough to be her father. She still dressed like a ragamuffin but had settled down to domestic life with him. It was a lifestyle that continued to include sadomasochism. Stephanie described in detail what transpired in this practice of sex. Apparently, she quite enjoyed the pain involved, and further related that there was an agreed-upon rule each participant pledged to follow. They had a safe word each partner would say when the pain went beyond their threshold and was no longer enjoyable. Once said, the partner delivering the pain stopped immediately.

After Stephanie departed, I was left with unsettling questions. I am no expert in this field and would not pretend to be. But our talk did cause me to ask myself how a sweet, innocent young lady could be so abused as a child that she chose pain in sex for enjoyment.

I refer to most sexually abused women and men as *innocent*. My belief is that the inappropriate sex acts forced on them caused a deficit in normal psychological, social, and relational growth.

You can compare it to a twelve-year-old attending a university and finishing a degree in two years. Now, at fourteen, the child has a BA degree. Intellectually, the child fits in college, but developmentally, a fourteen-year-old cannot satisfactorily socialize with young adults in their early twenties. A fourteen-year-old doesn't have the social skills of twenty-year-old adults.

Another question came to mind as I was taking a break from writing this book. Wouldn't it be grand if we all had a safe word so we could stop pain in our lives? Think how a safe

The Role of Pastoral Employee Counseling

word could be used in medicine, psychiatry, dentistry, surgery, terminal illness, and so many more painful times in life.

However, there is a flaw with this wishful fantasy. Stephanie's pain was self-inflicted by invitation because she desired it for pleasure. Most other pain in this world is inflicted on us and not by invitation, nor do we derive pleasure from it. Don't forget that the reason pain in all its forms exists in our world is because of sin. To discover the source of pain, we have to return to the Garden of Eden. It's in the Garden where we learn that we experience pain, just as Stephanie did, because of Adam and Eve's actions. In their choice to disobey God by taking forbidden fruit, they brought sin into the world. And as sons and daughters of Adam and Eve, we endure the pain of sin in our lives in all its forms.

But don't live in fear. Christians do have a safe word and his name is Jesus Christ.

By calling on Jesus Christ as their safe word, Christians learn how to cope with the pain of this life and will be free of all pain in the life to come in heaven.

2. Porcelain Skin and an Angel's Hands:

I will never forget the first day Erica came to see me. She was in her early twenties and her beauty was marked by two features—she had perfect skin, and her hands were delicate and soft.

As Erica revealed her story, I discovered her major issue was not liking her job. She had been with the company several years but had never found the job personally fulfilling. I asked her about college, and she admitted she'd attended for two years but dropped out. Life got in the way with bills to pay, and she didn't want to miss out on a social life. And then there was her boyfriend, which was another story.

I asked what she really wanted to do in life and she expressed she was not exactly sure. Then I probably surprised her with the direction I took the interview. I told her that she was a beautiful young woman and had amazing hands.

I asked if she'd ever thought of being a hand model? I mentioned several young ladies in the call center who did modeling on the side and found it to be quite lucrative.

I suggested that since she had a secure job at the call center, she could take her time to break into the industry. This suggestion would also give her a goal to work toward, taking her mind off her job. Once in the industry she would have options, whereas now she had none. Finally, I suggested a premise from which she should work. She needed to assess the natural assets which God had blessed her with and consider her beautiful skin and hands as a blessing.

Her face brightened up after having shed a few tears earlier. I have found that crying often relieves tension and anxiety. After drying her tears, her face glowed for a few moments with the idea. Erica admitted the idea of modeling had crossed her mind, but she'd not had someone like me with whom to discuss it. I could imagine the cogs in her brain turning. She acknowledged that it would take a great deal of work to prepare a portfolio. I reminded her that time was on her side and she had nothing to lose and everything to gain.

I could see by her face that although the idea momentarily ignited her imagination, she was afraid of failure. However, I did suggest that once in the modeling business, she would have more time to attend college, which did seem to appeal to her.

We ended the session with my suggestion that she think about it and that we talk at a later date. About a month later, she dropped by. Naturally, I asked if she had done anything related to our discussion. She replied no and quickly changed the subject. We discussed a variety of non-modeling topics, but she seemed happier when she left the office. Another month or two went by before she visited again. Same question. Same reply.

After this brief third encounter, she never returned. My thoughts were that although the idea of doing something different was appealing, she wasn't prepared to take the risk.

The Role of Pastoral Employee Counseling

Visiting me at random ceased being an encouraging time and had become shaded with guilt. Did I make a mistake in asking her about a change each time we briefly met? I may have, but I felt it was important to remind her that she was created for greater things in her life. "For we are God's workmanship, created in Christ Jesus to do good works, which God prepared in advance for us to do" (Eph 2:10).

In working with such a large number of employees, it stands to reason that some would deal with mental illness and addictions.

Examples of the War with Addiction and Mental Illness

There were several employees who were drug addicts and came to work high as kites. Their drug of choice temporarily alleviated the intense spiritual pain of believing their lives had no meaning. Even though they had jobs, life had no purpose because drugs had captured their freedom. I remember one woman in particular who was high most of the time, and she came to my office not because of me but because when I read the Bible to her, she received comfort. His Word literally turned madness into sanity, if only for an hour. I am convinced that she, along with several clients who exhibited symptoms of bipolar manic depression, were caught in a war for their souls. Some of these people were on street drugs to escape their mania, and others were off their prescribed medications for the same reason. Satan was using their vulnerable state of drug addiction or mental illness to pull them away from Jesus.

> Finally, be strong in the Lord and in his mighty power. Put on the full armor of God so that you can take your stand against the devil's schemes. For our struggle is not against flesh and blood, but against the rulers, against the authorities, against the powers of this dark world and against the spiritual forces of evil in the heavenly realms. Therefore put on the full armor of God, so that when the day of evil comes, you may be able to stand your ground, and after you have done everything, to stand. Stand firm then, with the belt of truth buckled around your waist,

with the breastplate of righteousness in place, and with your feet fitted with the readiness that comes from the gospel of peace. In addition to all this, take up the shield of faith, with which you can extinguish all the flaming arrows of the evil one. Take the helmet of salvation and the sword of the Spirit, which is the word of God. And pray in the Spirit on all occasions with all kinds of prayers and requests. With this in mind, be alert and always keep on praying for all the saints. (Eph 6:10–18)

Sadly, all of these clients ultimately ended up in residence in local psychiatric hospitals. During the first eighteen months of my presence on site, I averaged one forced hospitalization of an employee into a psychiatric facility per month. And by "forced," I mean the police had to come as well as an ambulance. Some of the employees went peacefully and others were handcuffed. Those who left voluntarily were transported by ambulance, and those that were taken by force left with the local police officers.

I will never forget an extraordinary and bizarre series of events that occurred on the day before Thanksgiving during my second year. No sooner had I entered my office at eight in the morning than I was called to a department where an employee was acting strangely and scaring employees around her. I had met her previously and knew she was diagnosed as bipolar. She was too agitated to stay at the facility, so I began the referral process to have her hospitalized.

Within seconds of returning to my office, I received another call from a different department. A second woman was acting out of character. She too was bipolar and agreed to be hospitalized. Back in my office after lunch, as if on cue, I received a third emergency call.

Three women all diagnosed as bipolar worked at three different sites on our campus. If I hadn't been there, I would not have believed it possible. These women were all very pleasant, hardworking employees, but each had not been taking their medications for the reason counselors most often hear: "I didn't think I needed my medication anymore because I was doing so well. I thought I could manage anything that might come up on my own." The three women had to be hospitalized as they were a danger to themselves and to other employees on campus. None of them resisted and all went to the hospital voluntarily. I spent the whole day expediting the procedures which are, by necessity, time-consuming.

These episodes illustrate one of the saddest aspects of mental illness. Victims of mental illness are not crazy, but have to deal with a lifetime burden the rest of the population does not understand. Unmedicated like these ladies, their behavior will change and may scare observers, but they need our help and not our critique. Sufferers of mental illness require our assistance and understanding, and not the assumption they are dangerous. The old saying "love conquers all" is true. Compassion and support are the ointment for the soul wounded by the dragon of mental illness.

And we know that in all things God works for the good of those who love him, who have been called according to his purpose.

ROMANS 8:28

— 4 —

God Made Mankind to Have Purpose

People Who Felt They Lacked Purpose

THE FIRST STORY IS about a young man I counseled on and off over a two-year period. Alec was handsome, in his middle to late thirties, and married to Linda, an attractive young woman who had a little girl who adored him. He was her idol because her biological father was in prison for life due to issues I cannot reveal here. All I need add is that the biological father's personal possessions were vastly more important to him than his daughter and wife.

Alec and Linda worked for the same company, had secure jobs, earned better than middle-class salaries, and because their employer was in the energy business, they had excellent health benefits. However, during our sessions, he revealed that his life was meaningless and he felt useless, hopeless, and of no value or importance—all symptoms of depression. On several occasions he told me word for word, "A monkey could do my job."

Yes, he was on antidepressant medication, but he would stop taking it for reasons only he understood and then resume the regimen when his wife or doctor learned he had stopped. He repeated this random cycle for as long as I'd known him. He was so convinced his life was without purpose that no matter what I suggested as an action plan for healthy change, he found a reason it would never work. I suggested he change departments at his company, or learn a new skill, or develop a new trade. He was intelligent, and although he had only a high school education, he had exceptional talent in computers, mechanics, law enforcement, and basic engineering.

I also brought to his attention that he was his stepdaughter's knight in shining armor. He was providing her a healthy father figure which would positively affect her life. However, none of these appeals to his fatherhood role dented his black armor of being a failure. Even discussing Linda, who adored him, had no effect. In his eyes, he was a failure to her, no matter how she appealed to him differently.

I received a call one day to the effect that this young man had gone missing over the weekend. Finally, very late on Sunday night, the security officer at a church noticed a truck parked in an isolated area of their lot, partially concealed by low-lying tree branches. The security guard could see a man inside the truck. He notified the police as he didn't want to contaminate the scene. When the police arrived, they broke the driver's door window and discovered that Alec had shot himself in the chest with a shotgun.

Prior to his suicide, he had given no indication to anyone, including his wife, that this was on his mind. We were all shocked, because although suicide was a major discussion topic in sessions with just the two of us and one time including his wife, he had concealed this plan to kill himself. I wish he had followed what David wrote in the book of Psalms: "I waited patiently for the Lord; he turned to me and heard my cry. He lifted me out of the slimy pit, out of the mud and mire; he set my feet on a rock and gave me a firm place to stand. He put a new song in my mouth, a hymn of praise to our God. Many will see and fear and put their trust in the Lord" (Ps 40:1–3).

The second story is about Irene, a lady in her late fifties to early sixties who had been depressed most of her adult life. As in my previous story, she too had a loving husband who had a good job that paid well. She did not have to work outside the home, lived in an upper middle-class neighborhood, and had nice clothes, jewelry, and loving adult children.

God Made Mankind to Have Purpose

During my discussions with Irene over the course of a year, I learned she had attempted suicide several times. Two previous attempts by asphyxiation in her garage with the car running were unsuccessful because her husband had arrived home early from work.

As in Alec's story, Irene was depressed because according to her, her life had no purpose. When we attempted to define purpose, she would go silent for long periods of time. During each session, she refused to engage in any constructive discussion. She continued to plunge deeper into her black hole. One Saturday, she reached the bottom and was ultimately successful in gassing herself in her garage.

Again, like the previous story, she had given no indications she was going to take her life. Her family had done everything to keep her alive, but a counselor learns in this business that when a client decides to take his or her life, there's no way of preventing the suicide. I wish she had read this passage and taken it to heart: "The Lord himself goes before you and will be with you; he will never leave you nor forsake you. Do not be afraid; do not be discouraged" (Deut 31:8).

The third story deals with depression and thoughts of suicide from a different aspect. During my first week with the company, an alert manager called saying she was concerned about one of her employees. I hurried to her department where one of the male team members had left a suicide note out in the open on his desk. We arranged for Jack and I to meet in a small conference room. He was a good-looking young man about twenty-five. He had a college education and his wife had a career job in another company.

As we talked, I learned Jack felt his life had no purpose or meaning. His job was not what he wanted, although he realized he was starting out in the work world and had to take what he could get. Thankfully, despite the note he had written and left on his desk, I discovered that he did not really want to die but was deeply depressed.

Due to the vigilance of the team manager, we were able to prevent Jack from fulfilling his stated intention. When I discussed the note with him, he was embarrassed and apologetic. I called his wife and she confronted him, asking why he had never shared such feelings with her. Based on professional standards, she took him to the emergency department of a hospital near their home. However, I must make an observation about the redemptive power of this couple's marriage. When Jack sat next to his wife and across the table from me, I was amazed at how her mere presence changed his demeanor. Her love, which seemed to radiate from her face, turned his depression upside down. While we talked, he revealed more aspects about his depression. He felt his life had no purpose because he was not fulfilling what he thought his role as husband should be. Although his depression had been a longstanding part of their marriage, he was blessed to have an understanding wife whose mere physical presence gave him the help he needed.

Here too, in this situation, I wish this young man could have understood David's words:

"Why are you downcast, O my soul? Why so disturbed within me? Put your hope in God, for I will yet praise him, my Savior and my God" (Ps 42:11).

You Do Have Purpose in Life

I hope by these three stories you can grasp that feeling as if your life has no purpose can ultimately lead to depression and suicide. However, I know your life has purpose because God placed it there before you were born. You may have experienced much of the abuse and shame I wrote about earlier, but God still has a purpose for you. I also know from counseling experience that it is from these abuses you can derive the strength to be a greater example of a person with purpose. In fact, you will have a stronger character than you thought possible because of your pain and suffering, heartache and disappointment, trials and tribulations. The apostle James explains why in the first chapter of his epistle in the New Testament: "Consider it pure joy, my brothers, whenever you face trials of many kinds, because you know that the testing of your faith develops perseverance. Perseverance must finish its work so that you may be mature and complete, not lacking anything" (Jas 1:2–4).

Who in their right minds would consider it pure joy in the face of hardship? James the apostle would. To understand why he wrote this admonition contrary to common sense, we have to turn to the Greek language of the New Testament. The Greek word used here and translated as "perseverance" comes from the same word used when gold and silver is smelted to eliminate their natural impurities. The intense heat melts the impurities out of the precious metals, leaving only the pure gold and silver.

Now you know why the apostle James urges Christians to consider life's ups and downs, losses and hardships, setbacks and restarts as periods of rejoicing! These heart-melting episodes are casting away our impurities to make us as humanly pure as possible before God. We don't understand these soul-wrenching incidents as they occur, but upon later reflection, we realize they were for a purpose—to make us reliant on God instead of ourselves so that we can learn to follow him one step at a time.

Having a Purpose is a Choice

Now let us go to the next step of examining how our free will determines our fate by understanding that purpose is a choice. God gives each person a purpose, but he does not force us to embrace it. He allows us to decide on our own whether to pick it up and run or to lay it aside. Similar to a TV game show, we can choose either door number one, which is God's purpose for our lives, or door number two, which is ignoring the purpose. Just like in the game show, we can only choose one door, and once chosen, we then have to live with the consequences. It seems evident that in the three stories I related, Alec and Irene chose door number two and the consequences were fatal. What about Jack? At first it seemed he was on his way to choosing door number two, but with his loving wife's support and medical intervention, he chose door number one.

There is a common theme in each of these individuals' lives. They are linked in spite of differences in their ages, backgrounds, and lifestyles. This common bond is that they chose *not* to have a purpose. I admit, I don't know all the details about their lives. And I don't know the severity of what they endured. But, like James wrote about with smelting out impurities, it would appear they did not use their life events to strengthen them. Each person had the choice to say to him- or herself over a period of time, "I am not going to give up! I am going to use this setback to make me stronger."

Here's the reason I know their choices weren't made in haste. When people encounter hardships, they either succeed in defeating them with determination over time, or they follow the alternative, easier path. With each additional hardship they encounter, they continue on the easy path and their wills grow weaker and weaker until the individual finally capitulates to life's hardships. This battle between the two choices has highs and lows in and of itself. I know some people who gave up and threw in the towel, but returned to the boxing ring a few years later, finished their match, and finally won.

My assessment might seem harsh, but let me explain. A quest for freedom to identify the purpose for your calling is a choice. It is the most demanding choice you will ever make, and once you are committed, your journey ahead will be frustrating. This journey's accomplishments will be the most satisfying fulfillment in life. "Do you see a man skilled in his work? He will serve before kings; he will not serve before obscure men" (Prov 22:29).

As we have seen, there are so many roadblocks to making the choice, and even more when you decide to pursue your quest. But Christians have an ally. "Commit to the Lord whatever you do, and your plans will succeed" (Prov 16:3).

You have a choice to buy a new car or to repair the old one. If you choose the second option, the money saved can be used toward the next semester's tuition. Do you have to buy your clothes at fancy stores in the mall, or can you shop at a retail chain and use the money saved toward paying down your credit card debt? By the way, I know many people who can afford expensive clothes and new cars but still choose to save money anyway.

God Made Mankind to Have Purpose

Read what David wrote: "The Lord delights in the way of the man whose steps he has made firm; though he stumbles, he will not fall, for the Lord upholds him with his hand" (Psalm 37:23–24).

People Who Made Choices

Here are two stories about people who pursued their arduous quest for freedom for their purpose and *found* their calling.

1. The Doctor:

    Several years ago, I saw a movie of a true-life story where a young lady had dyslexia. She had no academic support growing up, so she didn't learn she was dyslexic until she finished high school. She wanted to be a medical doctor, but with Cs and Ds in high school, she began college a mile behind everyone else. While in college, she learned how to study in spite of her dyslexia and improved her grades. However, she was denied entry to a medical school because her grade point average was not high enough.

    She told the medical school board of admissions she would return to college and retake every course she made a B in and ace them this time—which she did while working several jobs. Later, she returned to the board and overwhelmed them with her academic success and her never-give-up attitude. The movie ended by revealing that she finished medical school nearly at the top of her class and went on to become a top physician in her community—all achieved with no support from her family either monetarily or emotionally. "For I am the Lord, your God, who takes hold of your right hand and says to you, Do not fear; I will help you" (Isa 41:13).

2. The Cuban Mechanic's Twin Daughters:

    We lived in a small town in West Texas for about five years. I became friends with Miguel, a Cuban gentleman. He had brought his family to the US from Cuba during the ongoing dictatorship of Fidel Castro. Miguel was a talented mechanic. Other mechanics in the community were jealous of his skills and tried to run him out of business, but failed because he was an honest, decent, and dedicated mechanic. "Blessed are all who fear the Lord, who walk in his ways. You will eat the fruit of your labor; blessings and prosperity will be yours. Your wife will be like a fruitful vine within your house; your sons will be like olive shoots around your table. Thus is the man blessed who fears the Lord" (Ps 128:1–4).

Miguel's immigration story was fascinating. It took him fifteen years to set foot in the US. Most of the time was spent waiting his turn to be next in line for receiving his visa. He was a common man by societal standards, with no special social or political contacts, and he had no money to bribe anyone, so he waited. No telling how many times he made trips to the authorities or the number of phone calls he made before he was finally permitted passage.

Once he settled in the West Texas community, he had to wait a decade before his family was allowed to join him. His mid-teen daughters didn't speak English, but by their perseverance and with their father's support, by the time they graduated from high school, they were first and second in their graduating class. The girls were completely bilingual and were on the road to college with academic scholarships.

For those of you who feel so discouraged that you are about to throw in the towel on life, I want you to know you are not alone. Don't be intimidated by Miguel's story; instead, take heart and review another story in the Old Testament.

Joseph: Slave, Manager, Superintendent, Chancellor
(Genesis 37 & 39)

Joseph lived more than five thousand years ago in Canaan and then in Egypt. This was a time in ancient history when Egypt was the number-one nation of the known world. Joseph didn't know it, but his fate was about to determine Egypt's future.

God Made Mankind to Have Purpose

Why did God allow Joseph's brothers to sell him as a slave to the Ishmaelites of Midian? Why was he not worth more than twenty shekels of silver? Seems to me that the future leader of Egypt would be worth much more. All the brothers except Reuben decided to murder Joseph. What powers of communication did God give Reuben so he could convince his brothers not to murder Joseph? The brothers were persuaded against murder, but decided instead to throw Joseph into a cistern after beating him nearly to death.

Only by the grace of God did he survive the bone-breaking crunch as his body hit the stone floor. Or we could infer a different interpretation of this terrible event. Maybe God was grabbing Joseph's attention? Being beaten by his brothers, cast into a cistern, and then sold into slavery was the only way an arrogant, spoiled, entitled, selfish seventeen-year-old could be introduced to reality. Until this calamitous moment, Joseph had lived in a "preferred son" bubble. Blunt force trauma to Joseph's entire body was the only way God could shake him out of his prideful folly (Gen 37).

Just when Joseph thought life could not become any worse, he was sold to Potiphar, who was an "Egyptian, one of Pharaoh's officials, the captain of the guard" (Gen 37:36). Potiphar observed that whatever project Joseph was given always prospered. Therefore, he placed Joseph in charge of his entire home and lands. In fact, the Scriptures record that Joseph was so trustworthy, Potiphar no longer reviewed his personal accounts under Joseph's supervision.

Finally life was good for Joseph. But there was a snag. Potiphar's wife was a cougar who lusted after Joseph. However, although he was tempted in heart and flesh, he refused to sleep with her. One day all of Potiphar's servants and slaves were out of his house. The large dwelling was as quiet and peaceful as a cemetery at midnight. By reading between the lines of Scripture, we could infer that Potiphar's house being as empty as a mausoleum was no accident. Potiphar's wife, whose name we are never told, probably arranged for this timely solitude. She and Joseph were completely alone and now she had all the time she needed to seduce Joseph.

After much unsuccessful cajoling, Potiphar's wife was insulted and contemptuous. She turned her fury into revenge. The femme fatale side of her psyche emerged and she accused Joseph of raping her. The truth was the other way around. Joseph ran away from her so hastily he left his outer garment in her hand. Joseph was a handsome and well-built young man who could have slept with any slave or free woman of his desire, but he chose to honor God instead by his morality and chastity.

Joseph was quickly thrown into prison because Potiphar's wife presented his outer garment as evidence. She told her husband she was able to grab it as she hurried away from Joseph. She was never caught in her lie and deception. However, I've always thought that Potiphar knew his wife had a roving eye, and that this event with Joseph was not the first time scandal had filled Potiphar's house.

After many years of successful work, Joseph witnessed the fruit of his labor disappear as quickly as a rabbit down its burrow. To go from chief administrator of the second-highest man in Egypt to being a common criminal must have been a humiliating blow. Can you imagine how he felt? Joseph was made a jail bird for life because he followed his principles and made the right choice.

What would you do if you were in Joseph's shoes? You made the correct choice by fighting for your honor. You also thought you had God on your side to protect you. And you still wound up in prison, with no hope of parole or pardon.

Joseph could have spent the rest of his life in a dirty, unhygienic, rat-infested hole in the ground. Thousands of years ago prisons were not like they are today, with air conditioning and color TV. Worse yet, he had no lawyer or family to appeal to for help. He was totally alone—except for one person. This person had been with him all the time, watched over him when he slept, and watched his back. His name was Jehovah.

If you were in Joseph's sandals, what would you say to God? Let me offer a few suggestions. In anger, I would be asking, "What did I do wrong, God? Why am I being punished, God?" I probably would be spitting, hitting the walls with my fists, and shaking them up at God. Then when I rested a little from my violent, childish outburst, I would put it to God straight. "This is not right! You allowed me, your servant, to be punished because I did the right thing. God, you don't make a lot of sense. Why should I follow you, believe you, trust you?"

But guess what happened. "But while Joseph was there in the prison, the Lord was with him; he showed him kindness and granted him favor in the eyes of the prison warden. So the warden put Joseph in charge of all those held in prison, and he was made responsible for all that was done there. The warden paid no attention to anything under Joseph's care, because the Lord was with Joseph and gave him success in whatever he did" (Gen 39:20–23).

Seems we have heard similar words before. Well, the same thing happened there in prison as when Joseph was given charge over Potiphar's house. Again, we find Joseph in a situation not of his choosing, but one where God will refine and develop Joseph's character.

Some time passed. Joseph ran the prison efficiently, but he wanted his freedom. One day, Pharaoh's baker and cupbearer were placed in prison with Joseph. Somehow, they had offended Pharaoh.

After an undisclosed period of time, both men had a dream on the same night. They asked Joseph to interpret their dreams and he agreed. The cupbearer's dream revealed he would be released in three days and restored to his position. But the baker's dream revealed he would be executed in three days. These revealing truths left the cupbearer very happy and the baker fearful for his life.

Sure enough, Joseph's interpretations proved true: the baker was hung and his body was left to the crows to be eaten, while the cupbearer was restored to Pharaoh's side. Joseph asked the cupbearer to remember him when he returned to his position. Since Joseph continued to languish in prison, he probably figured the cupbearer had forgotten about him.

Once again it appeared that Joseph had been slapped in the face for doing what was right. I am unsure about you, but I think at this point I would have given up and said to God, "It's over. I'm tired of always doing the right thing only to be kicked in the teeth. Why bother with doing right when it gets me nowhere but only produces more disappointment?"

However, more time passed and then Pharaoh also had a dream. Suddenly, the cupbearer remembered Joseph's talent for dream interpretation. We are not told this in Scripture, but the cupbearer was probably not thinking of Joseph's welfare when he placed a word in Pharaoh's ear: "Hey Pharaoh, I know a guy in prison who can interpret your dream. Would you like me to contact him?"

Now, of course you know this seeming gesture of goodwill had a hidden agenda. The cupbearer was looking to be the hero of the day and perhaps receive some perks. Maybe another wife. Perhaps some riverfront acreage on the Nile. What about more slaves, or a new chariot for his two-chariot garage? Again, we are not told what happened to the cupbearer, but we are told how Joseph skyrocketed to the top of Egypt's royal social ladder.

Pharaoh's dream revealed that there would be seven years of abundance and bountiful harvests followed by seven years of famine. Pharaoh knew he was not an agriculture manager and needed to devote his time to ruling. He was shrewd and wise enough to know he needed to delegate this job to a good manager. That is how Joseph became the minister of agriculture in Egypt. Pharaoh announced that Joseph would be second to him in all of Egypt. As an added bonus, he gave Joseph his daughter, Asenath, for his wife.

Four Principles of Having Purpose Found in Joseph's Story

1. Trust:

    This story tells us of a Hebrew boy aged about thirty who became second-in-command over all Egypt, second only to Pharaoh. There is an additional phenomenon in this decision that defies hundreds, perhaps thousands of years of royal Egyptian birthright heritage. Pharaoh was considered a god on earth. He had the power of life and death over his subjects. His word was final in all matters. To defy Pharaoh or question him was to bring immediate death upon the questioner.

God Made Mankind to Have Purpose

What are we to think about this dirty Hebrew slave who was given the same status as Pharaoh? He smelled of prison. He needed a bath. You'd better stand downwind of him. The decision to elevate Joseph to the level of sovereign defies logic in Egyptian thinking. It questions all that is normal. It turns the Egyptian belief system upside down. Joseph was an alien and an outsider, and he was not divine in Egyptian eyes. And yet, there he was in a royal chariot with soldiers running in front of and behind him. He had servants and slaves by the hundreds at his beck and call twenty-four hours a day.

There is only one explanation for Joseph having ascended to this position. The promotion came from God. God placed Joseph where God had planned for him to be—not where the young man wanted to be or thought he deserved to be. However, for Joseph to understand the divine plan, God deemed it necessary for Joseph to have some apprenticeship training in the virtue of trust.

Here's another interesting observation: From the time Joseph was cast into the cistern until he became second-in-command of Egypt, we read no words of wavering, second guessing, or questioning God. I am sure most of us in his sandals would have wanted to know where God was taking us. I believe we also would have grumbled and complained, and even acted like children and thrown tempter tantrums. I, certainly, would have wanted to know why I kept running into dead ends.

What we do read is that each time Joseph hit a low point in his life, God used the experience to build Joseph's character. "Cast your cares on the Lord and he will sustain you; he will never let the righteous fall" (Ps 55:22).

I would like to delve a little deeper into the relationship between Joseph's trust and his character.

First, trust is built on adversity because adversity builds character. How, you might ask? Wouldn't God prove his trustworthiness by easing Joseph's life? Emphatically, no! Besides, this reasoning begs the question of who was in charge, God or Joseph? Joseph needed to learn to trust because he served God and not the other way around.

Let me use a simple illustration. Anthropologists of today have learned to sharpen flint into knives in the same manner as prehistoric man. Learning this refined technique took time, patience, and practice, along with many broken pieces of flint. The process of transforming a small piece of flint into a razor-sharp knife (perfect for removing a beard) is fascinating. This real-time transformation comes through adversity—striking a rock against the flint at just the right angles to form a refined blade.

This is how God uses adversity to create trust. He put Joseph through some real-time hardships, physical and emotional. God honed Joseph's character to be razor-sharp, trusted, and true, to such an extent that he was ready and able to slice through any adversity life presented.

Second, Joseph needed adversity in his life in order for him to build trust in God. Joseph was blinded by his humanity. He lacked vision, understanding, and a creative grasp of the circumstances within his surroundings. Joseph saw only failure and not the opportunity within the failure. In his weakness, he saw only darkness. Through his doom and gloom, he could not see the small rays of the eternal on his horizon.

By the time he became second-in-command to Pharaoh, he'd stopped seeing only the catastrophes in his life. Joseph's trust bloomed like the lotus flower on the Nile. "The Lord is a refuge for the oppressed, a stronghold in times of trouble. Those who know your name will trust in you, for you, Lord, have never forsaken those who seek you" (Ps 9:9–10).

2. Work:

Agriculturalists of today would agree that farming techniques in Egypt five millennia ago were primitive, to say the least. No machinery, just animals and slaves. And slaves were managed like animals. Think how a new slave, a Hebrew boy of about seventeen or eighteen, would be inspected as a newly acquired property. He appeared in good physical condition, but like any new livestock, he needed to be given a thorough physical examination.

First, one of the Egyptian farmhands probably grabbed Joseph's upper and lower jaw and forced him to open wide. Good teeth, a sign of good nutrition. Next, the farmhand probably thumped his biceps, shoulders, and thighs and noticed they were hard. Hands and feet passed muster, as did hearing and vision. Now the farmhand was sure Joseph had proven to be a good purchase.

This treatment may seem inhumane, but to the Egyptians, Joseph was chattel. He, along with a few other slaves in good shape, could pull a plow should the need arise.

Now think of how Joseph was treated by the other slaves who had seniority over him. I would imagine he was given the worst straw to sleep on when he was permitted to sleep. He was probably always the last in line to receive his food, so he ate the dregs from the pot. Whenever a thankless job came along, it was given to Joseph. And you can bet Joseph was beaten if he didn't perform well. "But if you suffer for doing good and you endure it, this is commendable before God" (1 Pet 2:20b).

Slaves formed a melting pot of nations the Egyptians had conquered. There would have been numerous languages to learn, including Egyptian. Think about how many times Joseph was beaten because he made the slightest mistake due to not understanding a language. Consider the pecking order of who was bullied or beaten just for fun.

There was no Equal Employment Opportunity Commission to appeal to if Joseph felt he was being treated unfairly by his employers. There was probably no recourse if he was injured. I would venture to say—knowing man's appetite for vengeance—that Joseph learned to keep his aches and pains and feelings to himself. He knew no one would listen to him anyway, so why bring up any issue for discussion? "For it is commendable if a man bears up under the pain of unjust suffering because he is conscious of God" (1 Pet 2:19).

We are not told how long Joseph was at the bottom of the labor pool, but we are told that God was with him and the young man soon rose through the different levels of management. However, his rise to power in Potiphar's house didn't happen overnight. He still had to work his way through the ranks. Joseph also had to overcome the jealousy and envy of other slaves who had been in the labor pool longer.

Joseph had to learn different languages, new farming techniques, and customs of other cultures. This all took time, and it was during this period that Joseph worked his way up to be number two in all of Potiphar's house. "Whatever you do, work at it with all your heart, as working for the Lord, not for men, since you know that you will receive an inheritance from the Lord as a reward. It is the Lord Christ you are serving" (Col 3:23–24).

I am sure there were times Joseph wanted to lay down and die because he saw other slaves murdered who gave up due to exhaustion. I am also sure he wanted to quit and run away. But where would he go? He wouldn't have had the resources to make a successful escape. I believe he saw the bodies of other slaves who'd tried to escape brought back hanging on poles like animal carcasses.

He had many sleepless nights, hungry days, cold winters, and hot summers. Joseph was probably so exhausted he could barely put one foot in font of the other. However, even in his weakest moments he continued to believe God had not abandoned him. "So we say with confidence, 'The Lord is my helper; I will not be afraid. What can man do to me?'" (Heb 13:6).

3. Sacrifice:

What did Joseph sacrifice? He had no money or personal valuable possessions. The only item he had was his fancy coat, and his five half brothers stole that. They spread animal blood on it and then took it to their father, Jacob, and lied to him, saying Joseph had been attacked by a wild animal from the desert.

Joseph had nothing tangible to sacrifice. Besides, possessions can be replaced, but what Joseph sacrificed were personality traits that needed to be removed from his life, never to be replaced but to be *exchanged*. God knew the only way for his sacrifice to occur.

Joseph sacrificed his *pride* for humility the first time he was hit by one of his half brothers. Joseph sacrificed his *ego* for modesty when his Midianite masters crossed his back with a whip, leaving numerous scars. He also sacrificed his ego when he wore chains around his ankles and wrists that cut deep into his skin, causing gaping wounds that bled all the way to Egypt.

Joseph sacrificed his *pretty-boy looks* for meekness when the dirt on the road whirled around him, caking in his eyes, nose, mouth, and ears. His pretty-boy looks were sacrificed the first time he was approached to perform sexual acts and he refused. This refusal ultimately led to him either being raped or beaten or both, since he was not trained to defend himself.

Joseph sacrificed his *arrogance* for modesty the first time he discovered that no one was bowing down to him, as he dreamed his brothers would do. And the only attention he received was when he was slapped across the face for not dropping to his knees quickly enough when his superiors entered into his presence.

He sacrificed being a spoiled rich kid and learned to serve others before himself. Joseph sacrificed living by his adolescent hormones to living by using his mind. And finally, Joseph sacrificed living for himself and learned to live for God. The only way he learned to practice virtue instead of vice was at the sacrificial altar of brutal life experience.

4. Overcoming fear:

Joseph had many fears to conquer. Seems he was in an ever-present whirlwind of fear. First, there was the fear of his brothers, who wanted to murder him; then the fear of the

Midianites, who purchased him as their slave. Potiphar was a man Joseph probably feared for many years. What about Potiphar's wife? How often had she tried to make Joseph sleep with her? Then there was the fear of the jail keeper, along with a vast horde of unsavory characters in prison. I would venture to say Joseph had to learn his way around, not showing his fear to murderers, thieves, swindlers, and cutthroats.

However, I believe his greatest fears where those that came from within. I am sure there was an initial panic that set in when he was beaten and thrown into the cistern. His father Jacob was no longer around to protect him. To whom could he turn? For the first time in his seventeen years of life, he was forced to trust in an "entity" he could not see, hear, touch, smell, or embrace.

During his thirteen-year sojourn in Egypt as his station in life went from bad to good and then to worse, he probably always feared tomorrow. He might have voiced these questions in regards to his fears: "Will I live until tomorrow morning? Will I live the remainder of this day? How will I face death? Will I meet death nobly, or will I be a coward?"

Did he show any kind of confidence while fear raged inside him as he lived as a slave? Was he afraid he would give in to lust even though he'd denied Potiphar's wife? Did he run out of the room to escape her, or did he flee because he was afraid that if he stayed a moment longer, he would give in to temptation?

Can you imagine the fear he must have felt the first day on the job working for Potiphar as his number-two man? Would it not also be safe to say he felt the same fear his first day on the job when he was placed in charge of the prison? Then finally, what was the depth of his fear when he began his first day on the job as Pharaoh's number-two man in all of Egypt?

I think that no matter how much he trusted God, Joseph was probably still riddled with fear because he knew he was an imperfect man.

God Made Mankind to Have Purpose

When we reflect on Joseph's climb up the Egyptian political and corporate ladders to become the number-two man in Egypt, we can see God's management training program. Joseph advanced from being a slave to having the life-or-death say over any citizen or noncitizen of Egypt. Each position prepared him for the next job. Ironically, Joseph never aspired to any of these jobs. Yet there he was, as close to being a king as he could possibly be in the most powerful nation of the known world.

Every day of his surprising life was a new day. Each was filled with choices and decisions he had to make. Not in his wildest dreams or vaguest hopes would he have chosen these jobs. I would say every day was a day of fear, but his life demonstrates that he was in constant communication with God.

When he rose in the morning before the sun and when he went to bed at night long after the moon was high in the sky, Joseph gave his fear to God. During these thirteen years, he learned in his daily challenges that God was his protector and not Jacob, his earthly father.

But I Don't Know My Purpose

You may be thinking, "Okay, Glenn I get it. My life does have a purpose and that purpose is in God. But how do I learn what that purpose is? I'm no Joseph. So how do I determine what God's purpose is for me?"

I answer this question in the next chapter.

The purposes of a man's heart are deep waters, but a man of understanding draws them out.

PROVERBS 20:5

— 5 —

How to Discover Purpose

Jonah, God's Conflicted and Complicated Prophet

A Story of Self-Inflicted Pain

JONAH WAS A THOUGHT-PROVOKING but common man. Before we profile the man, let me give you some geographical and historical guidelines. He lived in a small village called Gath-hepher northeast of Bethlehem. Oddly, the meaning of the name is "winepress of digging." How this name came about for this tiny community is up for grabs by archaeologists; however, this definition has no bearing on the story or the character of the man, Jonah. But since we're on the meaning of names, Jonah in the Hebrew language means "dove."

I don't know about you, but when I think of a dove, I think of peace, a truce or armistice, and even tranquility. A dove is often depicted with a small olive branch in its beak as a symbol of a cease-fire ending a war—symbols which have their origin from the time of Noah. God used the dove with an olive leaf in its beak to inform Noah that there was a truce between God and humanity: "When the dove returned to him in the evening, there in its beak was a freshly plucked olive leaf! Then Noah knew that the water had receded from the earth" (Gen 8:11).

Want to Get the Most out of Life?

When I learned the translation of Jonah's name, I thought it ironic. As his story and personality are revealed in the Scriptures, I think a more descriptive name for him would have been "bull." Jonah wanted to do the opposite of everything God told him to do. He was like a bull charging through a field in the wrong direction, ignoring peripheral vision while looking straight ahead at the red cape.

In my opinion, Jonah was self-centered and self-righteous. However, assessing his virtue using a different measure, he was unmatched in his devotion to Jehovah. Jonah had his own way of accomplishing a task as opposed to God's way to live his faith. As followers of the Great I Am, we cannot live unto ourselves alone. It would be like a citizen of the United States telling the president he was not going to follow American law but still wanted to be a US citizen.

In defense of Jonah's attitude, he might have felt that God needed help from him in some of his decisions. When it came to his covenant with God, Jonah, as a Jew, acted like a bull charging a matador determined to celebrate as he gored his human adversary. And Lord help anyone who got in Jonah's way.

At the beginning of the story, Jonah was quietly going about his life with no aspirations to be a prophet for Jehovah. But lo and behold, God spoke to Jonah: "Leave your home in Gath-hepher and travel to Assyria to the city of Nineveh."

Ever the skeptic, Jonah asked why.

"Go to the great city of Nineveh and preach against it, because its wickedness has come up before me" (Jonah 1:2).

We need to pause here and examine the statement "its wickedness has come up before me." What would the typical Christian think after reading this phrase? Most of us would assume it's an expression of God's anger and disappointment in humanity, and continue reading. Well, you are partially correct. Here are three examples to emphasize this point.

First, Cain and Abel:

> Now Cain said to Abel, "Let's go out to the field." And while they were in the field, Cain attacked his brother

Abel and killed him. Then the Lord said to Cain, "Where is your brother Abel?" "I don't know," he replied. "Am I my brother's keeper?" The Lord said, "What have you done? Listen! Your brother's blood cries out to me from the ground. Now you are under a curse and driven from the ground, which opened its mouth to receive your brother's blood from your hand. When you work the ground, it will no longer yield its crops for you. You will be a restless wanderer on the earth." (Gen 4:8–12)

Notice what God said to Cain: "Your brother's blood cries out to me from the ground."

Second, Noah and the flood:

> The Lord saw how great man's wickedness on the earth had become, and that every inclination of his heart was only evil all the time. The Lord was grieved that he had made man on earth, and his heart was filled with pain. So, the Lord said, "I will wipe mankind, whom I have created, from the face of the earth—men and animals, and creatures that move along the ground, and birds of the air—for I am grieved that I have made them." But Noah found favor in the eyes of the Lord. (Gen 6:5–8)

Notice what the passage says: "The Lord saw how great man's wickedness on earth had become, and that every inclination of his heart was only evil all the time." Later we read from the Scriptures that in spite of man's wickedness, God was willing to forgive him.

Third, Sodom and Gomorrah:

> Then the Lord said, "The outcry against Sodom and Gomorrah is so great and their sin so grievous that I will go down and see if what they have done is as bad as the outcry that has reached me. If not, I will know." (Gen 18:20–21)

These three episodes in Hebrew history reveal a patient and kind God that man does not deserve or understand. "Praise be to the Lord, to God our Savior, who daily bears our burdens. Our God is a God who saves; from the Sovereign Lord comes escape from death" (Ps 68:19–20).

Another nugget we can draw from these stories is that when God first sees man, cities, or even nations overtly sin without regret or shame, he does not immediately punish them. God waits to discipline, whereas if we were in God's place, we would not have waited to punish man. Why does God wait? Is it because he condones what rises up before him in heaven? No! He waits because as we read in all three stories, he is patient to a point. Then once man reaches a certain level of sin, he acts.

In many instances, God sends a prophet or other messenger—like Noah, who built the ark to give people a warning. Most of the time, the people to whom the warning is given do not heed the message, as we see with Sodom and Gomorrah and with Noah and the flood. "The Lord is not slow in keeping his promise, as some understand slowness. He is patient with you, not wanting anyone to perish, but everyone to come to repentance" (2 Pet 3:9).

People often ask where God draws sin's red line in the sand. No human knows, but if you examine these and other stories in history, you'll see that God allows man to become fairly corrupt before he acts. However, once God acts, there is *no* turning back. Remember Lot's wife, who turned into a pillar of salt for looking back at Sodom as it was destroyed (Gen 19:26). God means what he says. We should never question his sovereign mercy, his grace, or his final word.

Evidently the phrase "man's wickedness comes before God" means he will not tolerate the evil any longer. He is not so much angry as hurt because as a father, he does not enjoy punishing his children, but there are times he must act—when the anger behind the hurt has reached its boiling point.

Unlike human fathers, God does not lash out impulsively or spontaneously. His punishment is measured, just, and final. "My son, do not despise the Lord's discipline and do not resent his rebuke, because the Lord disciplines those he loves, as a father the son he delights in" (Prov 3:11–12).

The Assyrians were a brutal people who sacrificed captives, slaves, and malcontents as easily as we would step on a bug. They also regularly sacrificed human beings to their gods, including children and babies. Time and paper do not permit me to write about the other brutal tortures they inflicted as regularly as we take out the day's trash. If you're interested in carrying this subject further, read the book of Nahum from the Old Testament.

Remember that Jonah was sent to Nineveh, an Assyrian city. Not only did the Assyrians murder, rape, pillage, and plunder, they also practiced incest, homosexuality, and probably a host of other sexual perversions. These were all practiced in the name of their religions. They had male and female prostitute priests and priestesses who were hired for the purpose of worship, paid for by animal sacrifices.

Finally, the citizens of Nineveh had crossed the red line of sin drawn in the sand. God wanted Jonah to go to Nineveh to preach repentance. If they listened to Jonah, then God would withdraw his red line and forgive them. "The Lord is gracious and compassionate, slow to anger and rich in love. The Lord is good to all; he has compassion on all he has made" (Ps 145:8–9).

There is dark humor in this command from God to Jonah. Not because God's command is funny. No one should disobey or take God's commands as anything but serious. Like the time God told Abraham to sacrifice Isaac, his only son. Abraham didn't understand this command, but he obeyed it (Gen 22:1–18).

No, the dark humor to me reading between the lines is found in Jonah 1:3. In a story of this magnitude, we should have been told that he packed his bags and began his journey. After all, Nineveh, with all its 120,000 citizens steeped in sin, was a five-hundred-mile walk inland northeast of his home.

Instead of obeying God, we read that Jonah headed south to Joppa, where he boarded a boat bound for Tarshish in the southern area of Spain, nearly three thousand miles away by sea. But God had other plans. Jonah never completed this journey. Instead, the boat was buffeted by raging storms and Jonah had to jump overboard, then he was swallowed by a large fish!

I find it interesting in that there is no dialogue recorded between Jonah and God concerning Jonah's disobedience. Many prophets did not agree with God initially, but they had open and honest discussions with God. God rarely changed his mind and then his prophet fulfilled his command as originally given, with commitment as a result of their discussion.

Here is the answer to my query: "But Jonah ran away from the Lord" (Jonah 1:3). This phrase tells us a great deal about Jonah the man. Here's why. Can any human "run away from God?" Read Psalm 139 and you will discover the answer, because no one can escape God. Then why did Jonah behave like a child and run away, especially when he knew he could not escape God? This is where Jonah's childish passive-aggression raised its ugly head. Instead of being a man and behaving like Moses did when he disagreed with God, Jonah ran away like a child without saying a word. I bet he even left at night thinking he could avoid being seen by God.

Why was Jonah's heart not set on God's mission? Jonah knew God was fair and just and that if he followed the command to preach the message of repentance, Nineveh might repent. In his sanctimonious mind, Jonah knew God would do the unthinkable and forgive the Ninevites. And in his spiritual self-righteousness, Jonah didn't want the Ninevites to have a chance to repent.

This decision of grace and mercy extended the red line of sin too far for Jonah. He wanted to see God utterly destroy Nineveh down to the last man, woman, and child. He believed Nineveh deserved no forgiveness. Death was their just reward because of their reprehensible behavior. Perhaps this is the point where Jonah thought God was being a little too kind and needed to rethink his decision.

Instead of being tough on Jonah, I think it's fitting for me to ask myself whether or not I act any differently in my faith than Jonah. My answer is an emphatic no. I am just as shallow and spiritually weak, and I refuse to have an honest discussion with God today. I know I should get on my knees to pray about an issue, but do I? No, because like Jonah, I have my own Joppa I can escape to. I also have my own personal Tarshish where I can hide.

Like Jonah, I run west when I should be headed east. Why? Because I already know God's answer before I ask him. And I am not running away from God but from myself—because I won't like

God's answer. Similar to Jonah, I refuse to embrace the reality of God's choice, whether it be forgiveness, mercy, grace, or kindness. At the heart of this escape is my idea of justice taking precedence over God's justice.

No sooner had Jonah's ship set sail to the west than a storm broke out. The Scriptures record the event: "Then the Lord sent a great wind on the sea, and such a violent storm arose that the ship threatened to break up" (Jonah 1:4). The storm was so violent that the sailors threw all the cargo overboard to lighten the load. Everyone on board was so sure they were going down with the ship that each sailor prayed to his own god for deliverance. They looked for Jonah and couldn't find him. Then the captain went below deck, and finally found Jonah sound asleep.

The captain was incensed and flabbergasted. He confronted Jonah and asked how he could sleep at a time like this. The captain pleaded for Jonah to call on his God to deliver the captain and his crew. Jonah had the answer to prevent their impending drowning. I doubt the captain had ever heard a plea like this before. Jonah advised them to throw him overboard, but the crew refused. How could murdering an innocent man save them?

In disobedience to Jonah's solution and God's command, they attempted to row the boat closer to shore. But the storm increased in severity. Finally, they threw Jonah overboard and instantly the storm subsided. The sailors worshiped Jonah's God and vowed to live better lives to honor their deliverance.

At this sudden change of events, God provided a large fish to swallow Jonah. Jonah was in the belly of the fish for three days. The fish disgorged Jonah onto the shore, and Jonah made his way to Nineveh. There in Nineveh Jonah issued the Lord's prophecy of repentance.

While Jonah was in the belly of the fish for three days, he had a change of heart. A slight change of heart. Yes, he did spend three days preaching to the citizens of Nineveh to repent. When they did, Jonah should have been ecstatic. But instead, he became angry and set up camp outside the city, watching and hoping God had changed his mind and would destroy Nineveh. However, Jonah's desire was not fulfilled. His anger increased—so much so that he chastised the Lord. Personally, I've not read of anyone who confronted God and lived to see another day. Yet God allowed Jonah to live because the man had not fulfilled his purpose.

That is not the end of Jonah's story. While he waited for Nineveh's destruction in his camp east of the city, God planted a vine that grew quickly and provided Jonah with shade. But as Jonah's luck would have it, the vine died. Within a two-day period, the vine grew and provided shade, but then a worm ate the vine. Now Jonah became even more livid at God. God didn't punish Nineveh and he took away Jonah's shade.

God then counseled Jonah by asking a simple question. And God was hoping Jonah would get over himself and his elephant-sized pride. God asked (and I'm paraphrasing), "If I provided a vine to give you shade and then took it away in order for you to witness my power, how can you question my concern for Nineveh, a city of one hundred and twenty thousand souls?" In other words, how much more should God be merciful to their sins than he was to Jonah's discomfort in the heat?

We Can Learn Our Purpose through Jonah's Calling

Jonah is the last person in the world other writers would use to illustrate how to learn one's purpose in life. I can think of many other examples of men and women in the Old and New Testaments who exhibit better illustrations.

David, who was "a man after God's own heart," would be the best choice. Then there is Jonathan, David's best friend and Saul's son. Jonathan was conflicted in loyalty between David and King Saul. This personal conflict arose because Saul hated David, but David and Jonathan loved each other. They had fought the Philistines as comrades in arms, hunted wild beasts, and chased the same girls.

Then there is Deborah of the Old Testament, who lead Israel against the cruel King Jabin of Hazor, a Canaanite. And there are many more. However, it's precisely because Jonah is nearly the worst example to learn one's life purpose from that I chose him.

Jonah is not only a study in conflict, but a study in contrasts. What can we learn about discovering our God-given purpose from a shallow, superficial, self-righteous Jew called to be a prophet? Here are five noteworthy principles.

1. We Don't Have to Be Perfect:

    People in the counseling profession encounter many clients who feel they have to be perfect in their careers or life. These people think that if they are not number one in their classes, they are a failure. They are intimidated by others who make better grades, those who perhaps don't have to study as hard, or those who have a genetic predisposition for memory or analytical ability.

    They compare themselves to these fellow classmates and give up hope, so they drop out of class and eventually school. Sometimes this inferiority spills over into social and economic opportunities they think others have which they don't. What do they do? They assume that without these benefits they may as well not try before they even start.

    Take a close look at Jonah. He was selfish, self-centered, highly self-righteous, and entitled as a Jew. The Ninevites were so beneath him they deserved their punishment. Note this was Jonah's chastisement and not God's. Don't you think God should have chosen another Jew with better credentials to be his prophet? Jonah would not be on my A list for admission to the School of Prophetic Training. He would have never made my list at all. His virtues were anything but stellar.

    Nonetheless, God chose Jonah to be his prophet to Nineveh. This choice is the best example God gives about having a purpose—*none of us is perfect*. Let us all take comfort in this fact. As we see in Jonah's life, we don't even have to be willing.

Want to Get the Most out of Life?

I've met many counselees who hated their life-purpose. But as they began living their purpose, they discovered they were good at it, which surprised them. In truth, many didn't know they had the skills for their life's purpose when they began. Then the more they practiced their skills, the better they became as they sharpened and refined their talents. Let me give you an example.

I watched a program on TV several years ago about a highly successful and rich young businessman. Here's how he succeeded so well. While attending college to get a business degree, he worked part-time managing a downtown parking lot in a major city. He was the guy who issued the ticket when you arrived and told you where to park your car. Before you left, you'd pay him the fee owed.

He was a conscientious worker and learned the job well. When he finished college, he found out there was a downtown parking lot for sale, so he purchased it. Then he purchased a second lot and later a third. When the story of his business success aired, he owned so many lots that he had many employees managing them while he expanded his business. He told the interviewer it was never his intent to own parking lots.

He thought that with his degree all he had to do was apply for jobs with corporations and wait until he was hired. But while he waited, the first opportunity to purchase a lot almost fell into his lap. And the more he rolled up his sleeves and worked just like the rest of his employees, the more successful he became. If he was offered a deal to sell his business, he said he would never do it because he loved it so much.

Here's another interesting reality aligned with this story of success. Like this young man I told you about, other successful people I've met were not the best in their academic classes. There were many classmates or apprentices who made better grades and were smarter and sharper. Some folks with whom I talked didn't attend college or graduate school, but instead attended a community college for only two years.

How to Discover Purpose

Many didn't have college degrees but learned and got qualified or certified as they worked. They also discovered it wasn't always the smartest people who were successful, but the ones who were willing to work the hardest.

Sure, inspiration is great, but without perspiration, inspiration can only take you so far. A college professor told a class I was in several decades ago an axiom I've never forgotten, and it has proven to be true. He said the A students generally end up in life working for the C students. Why? Because C students learn a powerful work ethic—they never give up!

2. We Cannot Hide from Our Purpose:

Like Jonah, we can run from our purpose in life, but we can't hide. However, while trying to hide from our purpose we make our lives and those around us miserable. Why? Because a lifetime is wasted in mediocrity. I have counseled many clients who, deep inside, knew their purpose but were afraid to pursue it, so they went the safe route and achieved little.

Like Jonah, they ran from what was really happening in their hearts but weren't willing to face it. Jonah was not running from God, nor were these counselees who spent a lifetime in mediocrity—they were running from themselves. Jonah didn't want to face God, who wanted to give Nineveh a second chance. In the same manner, these counselees didn't want to face the fear of failure. Jonah and these clients were running from two different internal dilemmas, but for the same reason.

Jonah learned, however, that no one can run from God.

> Where can I go from your Spirit? Where can I flee from your Presence? If I go up to the heavens, you are there; if I make my bed in the depth, you are there. If I rise on the wings of the dawn, if I settle on the far side of the sea, even there your hand will guide me, your right hand will hold me fast. If I say, "Surely the darkness will hide me and the light become night around me," even the darkness will not be dark to you; the night will shine like the day, for darkness is as light to you. (Ps 139:7–12)

Want to Get the Most out of Life?

"Nothing in all creation is hidden from God's sight. Everything is uncovered and laid bare before the eyes of him to whom we must give account" (Heb 4:13).

"'Am I only a God nearby,' declares the Lord, 'and not a God far away? Can anyone hide in secret places so that I cannot see him?' declares the Lord, 'Do not I fill heaven and earth?' declares the Lord" (Jer 23:23–24).

"They called to the mountains and the rocks, 'Fall on us and hide us from the face of him who sits on the throne and from the wrath of the Lamb! For the great day of their wrath has come, and who can stand?'" (Rev 6:16).

3. Our Greatest Adversary Is from Within:

Why did a little-known Jewish prophet run the opposite direction from where he was called to preach? Why does an alcoholic drown his conscious life in an ocean of alcohol? Why does a drug addict slip into a deep coma of a temporary subconscious fantasy world? Why doesn't an abusive husband break the cycle of physically abusing his wife and stop emulating his father, who abused his mother? Why doesn't a sexual predator break the cycle of sexually abusing children as he was abused? Why does a man or woman drop out of college or graduate school and not return?

Each group of people I just mentioned share a common connection that is at the center of their struggles. Yes, human pride is swollen beyond capacity because they don't want to admit they need help. Their egos are bruised because they are ashamed of having their problems. And finally, they are deeply embarrassed to admit they have a problem they don't want to face. As a result, they each blame other people in their lives for their problems, making others the scapegoats for not facing themselves.

Over the years, I have counseled thousands of people from all ethnicities and socioeconomic levels. Each of them was facing the issues I listed above and many others. One day after years of counseling, I realized I was missing a major facet in diagnoses. I felt quite the fool since I had not seen it before. Many people who are addicted to alcohol, drugs, sexual misconduct may say they want to change, but they soon realize that change will be difficult and they are not willing to put forth the necessary effort. They may have to give up a lifestyle, or friends, or even a career, and choose not to.

There are several character traits these people share. One, a weak ego demanding everything be done his way. This demand covers up his fear of someone with a better idea. Two, a need to bully those around him so he can feel superior. Since he is a bully, no one will challenge him, so his weakness does not have to be confronted and changed. Three, an individual who is scared all the time, constantly belittles those around him because he is afraid they will discover he is not as strong as he portrays. Four, an individual who requires that all tasks be done by his instruction only. He rails against independent and objective thought because he is either fearful that others will discover he is in over his head, or in truth, he doesn't really know what he is doing.

If intervention is not forthcoming in the lives of these types of personalities, marriages will crumble, addictions start, their adult children abandon them, affairs are unfulfilling and frequent, and there will never be enough money no matter how rich they become. Accomplishment loses its value no matter how big, powerful, or successful. However, if they are unsuccessful, they will usually spend money like there is no tomorrow to cover up the financial insolvency.

I have seen these people I mentioned earlier become angry at life and unsuccessfully run away from submitting their wills to God. They also spend thousands of dollars on secular therapy and treatment centers without achieving genuine change. However, the few who are successful in changing their lifestyles do so by trading their broken wills for God's healing in their lives. They confess to God that they need his help and cannot change without him living in their lives.

Want to Get the Most out of Life?

Here is a perfect example in a true story of a dear friend. Robert was raised in East Los Angeles. He was small in stature, so he either fought or capitulated. He became a "scrapper," fighting anyone who attempted to mistreat him. Robert refused to join a gang because he was smart enough to see that gang members either died young or went to prison.

To add insult to injury, he never had a father figure in his life. He had several stepfathers but he never had a relationship with them. To even use the word "father" for these men was a stretch, especially since some of them abused him.

Robert taught himself to become a mechanic. Over the years, he became so good he repaired both street and race cars and earned a better living than many mechanics with official credentials. However, he also became addicted to snorting cocaine. After a decade of this lifestyle, he met a Christian street preacher who invited him to his church service. Robert attended because he knew he needed to make positive changes in his life but realized he couldn't do it alone. That night, this street preacher challenged him to stop snorting cocaine and to become a Christian.

The Holy Spirit worked with Robert that night. He never used cocaine again, and twenty-five years later when I met him, he was still clean. Robert had no therapy or counseling, and he never attended an inpatient treatment facility. He did what you are about to read in the apostle Paul's story. Today my friend has a wife and two beautiful and intelligent daughters. He is a preacher for a large church in San Antonio, Texas. I love this man as though he were my biological brother. I would compare our friendship to the love David and Jonathan had as found in the Old Testament. Now read about Paul's choice to reach out from within and give his will in submission to God's will.

Paul lamented about a thorn in his flesh. He had a conversation with God and requested that the thorn be removed. Paul gives us God's reply: "But he said to me, 'My grace is sufficient for you, for my power is made perfect in weakness.'

Therefore, I will boast all the more gladly about my weaknesses, so that Christ's power may rest on me. That is why, for Christ's sake, I delight in weaknesses, in insults, in hardships, in persecutions, in difficulties. For when I am weak, then I am strong" (2 Cor 12:9–10).

Here are a few more scriptures to help encourage us to turn to God and stop running from our life's purpose.

> Therefore we do not lose heart. Though outwardly we are wasting away, yet inwardly we are being renewed day by day. For our light and momentary troubles are achieving for us an eternal glory that far outweighs them all. So we fix our eyes not on what is seen, but on what is unseen. For what is seen is temporary, but what is unseen is eternal. (2 Cor 4:16–18)

> Submit to God and be at peace with him; in this way prosperity will come to you. Accept instruction from his mouth and lay up his words in your heart. If you return to the Almighty, you will be restored: If you remove wickedness far from your tent and assign your nuggets to the dust, your gold of Ophir to the rocks in the ravines, then the Almighty will be your gold, the choicest silver for you. Surely then you will find delight in the Almighty and will lift up your face to God. You will pray to him, and he will hear you, and you will fulfill your vows. What you decide on will be done, and light will shine on your ways. When men are brought low and you say, 'Lift them up!' then he will save the downcast. He will deliver even one who is not innocent, who will be delivered through the cleanness of your hands. (Job 22:21–30)

> Do not conform any longer to the pattern of this world, but be transformed by the renewing of your mind. Then you will be able to test and approve what God's will is— his good, pleasing and perfect will. (Rom 12:2)

> Teach me to do your will, for you are my God; may your good Spirit lead me on level ground. (Ps 143:10)

4. God's Love is Greater Than Our Fear:

What was Jonah's greatest fear when called by God?

Was he fearful of failing God's calling? No, because he knew God had elected him to preach to all of Nineveh.

Was he afraid he didn't possess the skills of public speaking, as Moses believed when God called him? "Moses said to the Lord, 'O Lord, I have never been eloquent, neither in the past nor since you have spoken to your servant. I am slow of speech and tongue'" (Exod 4:10). No, Jonah knew God would help him as he had helped other prophets in their speaking publicly.

Was Jonah afraid the Ninevites would execute him after his preaching? No, because he knew God would protect him, but he also knew that if God chose not to protect him there was a higher reason than mortal understanding. Either way, in life or death he knew that to be God's prophet had its risks. "For none of us lives to himself alone and none of us dies to himself alone. If we live, we live to the Lord; and if we die, we die to the Lord. So, whether we live or die, we belong to the Lord" (Rom 14:7–8).

Jonah's greatest fear was Nineveh's possible repentance. Their repentance would not be due to Jonah's distinguished public oration. He knew every word he preached would be as God had spoken it because his Holy Spirit would guide his tongue. Here then lies his conflicted state. Jonah knew God could do as he chose because he was God, and God was right to offer Nineveh a second chance, no matter what the lowly prophet thought. This is the heart of Jonah's inner moral dilemma. "If you, O Lord, kept a record of sins, O Lord, who could stand? But with you there is forgiveness; therefore you are feared" (Ps 130:3–4).

Jonah wanted all 120,000 citizens of Nineveh to die, including cattle, sheep, goats, and other domestic animals. He wanted none of the inhabitants, man or animal, to have a second chance. He had judged them in his heart and found them guilty, and they deserved justice, not mercy. A scorched earth policy as God had inflicted on Sodom and Gomorrah was the only appropriate solution in Jonah's mind.

Technically, Jonah was right, because the citizenry of Nineveh was barbaric and hedonistic. But here is the heart of Jonah's conflict. God chose mercy over justice. Jonah either would not or could not have an honest discussion with God about mercy, so he ran away.

But no matter how far he chose to run, he still ended up in Nineveh preaching. Even when he completed his prophetic message that Nineveh would be destroyed if the citizens didn't repent, he camped outside the city and waited for God to destroy it. Here again we see his conflicted faith. He obeyed God and preached, but was waiting and hoping God might change his mind. "Seek the Lord while he may be found; call on him while he is near. Let the wicked forsake his way and the evil man his thoughts. Let him turn to the Lord, and he will have mercy on him, and to our God, for he will freely pardon" (Isa 55:6–7).

I believe this story illustrates the depth and breadth of God's love in how he chose mercy over justice. He not only graced Nineveh with his mercy but graced Jonah as well. How? As much as Jonah wanted Nineveh to be punished for its moral sin, Jonah deserved equal punishment for his sin of self-righteousness. If we were to put a ruler next to these two sins, Jonah's self-righteousness would be equal in length to Nineveh's immorality.

Here is my rationale for this conclusion. With God, sin exists in many forms, from overt, vile immorality to pious, self-righteous self-absorption. However, the overt practice of each sin is not what eats away at the sanctity of the heart. Refer back to the measuring of Jonah's and Nineveh's sin. They were different but each was just as vile. In God's eyes, sin is sin. There are no big sins or little sins.

In simple terms, it's like having two hunting dogs of different breeds. They both have different hunting methods, but the prey will be just as dead no matter which dog attacks it first.

Want to Get the Most out of Life?

Please bear with me as I explain the depth of these issues. By his behavior, Jonah demonstrated that he lacked love. He practiced an inflexible, rigid conviction that everything was black or white with no room for gray. People like Jonah are critical of others because they are first critical of themselves. In their religious profile, forgiveness, patience, and grace are words they know by definition, yet personally they don't exhibit these virtues.

This is why these types of people don't have many relationships, and the relationships they do have are unstable and shaky at best because no one likes being constantly criticized. Spiritual insecurity is at the root of all they practice, because it is like a baseball bat they can swing with effect to beat down others with whom they disagree in an effort to uplift themselves.

Their religion becomes an ego compensation for low spiritual self-esteem. They have to be right at all times and in all things. Sad to say, people like Jonah usually come from homes where their fathers were just as critical. Perfection is all they know and since no one is perfect, these people have an unhealthy definition of perfection.

God's love, though, is greater than our greatest fear that prevents us from discovering our purpose in life. In my counseling career and in life, I have met many Jonahs who exhibit this same type of fear. They can never let down their guard because they feel people will realize they are afraid. These people are always living on a razor's edge, afraid that someone will learn how insecure they are in life. Like Jonah, they won't talk to anyone because to face the truth of being wrong is too overwhelming.

Here is another spiritual axiom. When we forgive ourselves, we learn to forgive others. We cannot practice these virtues on others first and then ourselves second. Forgiveness does not work like that. Look at Jesus's answer when a Jewish holy man asked, "Which is the greatest, the most important commandment?"

"'The most important one,' answered Jesus, 'Is this: 'Hear, O Israel, the Lord our God, the Lord is one. Love the Lord your God with all your heart and with all your soul and with all your mind and with all your strength.' The second is this: 'Love your neighbor as yourself.' There is no commandment greater than these'" (Mark 12:28–31).

The principle of forgiving oneself before forgiving others is essential to fulfilling one's purpose in life because we all will make mistakes along the path. We will have relationships where we will have to forgive others as they forgive us. This principle can be summed up in a passage from Micah: "He has showed you, O man, what is good. And what does the Lord require of you? To act justly and to love mercy and to walk humbly with your God" (Mic 6:8).

5. God Embraces Virtues Over Faults:

   What I love about the story of Jonah is that in spite of his weaknesses, he has one incredible virtue. He wasn't special—he was just a man and he was certainly flawed. However, his one strength was off the charts. He eventually traveled to Nineveh and preached repentance even though he didn't want to. It took Jonah a long time to reach the city, and as an outsider, he could have been killed, but he slogged onward and accomplished his purpose. People focus on our faults, so we too usually focus on our faults. However, we have a God who embraces our virtues, and we need to treat other people the same way.

   The best principle to follow for change is very easy to execute. When dealing with our children, employees, peers, or the man on the street, identify each person's strengths and focus on praising, boasting about, and rewarding them. This encouragement needs to be private and public. The child and the adult, as well as the child in the adult, will beam like the sun. And here is how.

   Every time you are around a man I'll call Stan, you find a legitimate reason to praise him publicly and privately. You will notice his self-image begin to change. By this practice I don't mean you should be untruthful about a strength he clearly does not possess. If you are fraudulent in your declarations of praise, in time Stan will realize you are not being genuine, and you will unintentionally damage his ego.

Look for his actual virtues and explore them with him. Ask Stan if he is aware of these virtues or if he has plans to develop them. If the man is married, arrange to have his wife present when you compliment him. My reason is that she will confirm your observations by saying, "I've been telling you this, honey, for as long as we have known each other." Men won't pay attention to their wives about their virtues because they think they are just being nice. However, when a male friend confirms what she has been saying, he will start to pay attention.

Let me tell you a true story. Several years ago, Chuck and Amy came for marriage counseling. Their presenting problem was far overshadowed by his personal problem of not seeing himself as a person of worth. During our discussions, I discovered he was a very intelligent young man who had been told throughout his life he had no worth as a person. He'd been brainwashed by his parents. He was told over and over that he didn't have the IQ to attend college and that he would fail, wasting time and money.

Amy was his savior. Here was a beautiful young woman with a college education who repeatedly told him he was smart. However, he didn't believe her or accept her opinion. I determined that he had fulfilled the failure prophecy of his family. Chuck was now at a crossroads. He had no formal education or training for a trade and his wife was pregnant.

During our time together, I learned he had an aptitude for mechanics. I also felt he needed a success under his belt. I suggested that he join the army and allow them to train him in mechanics at the government's expense. He balked at first because his immediate response was that he would fail. I again suggested that this was precisely why he should join.

He needed the accomplishment of completing boot camp under his career belt to launch him on a skyward path to success in life. After much discussion, he signed up and passed boot camp. I was honored to be invited to the ceremony and was as proud of him as though he were my own son. Chuck did specialize in auto mechanics, and later, when he left the army, he attended a highly specialized civilian diesel big rig truck course for two years, and now has a great job as a diesel mechanic.

You are probably scratching your head and asking yourself, What does this story have to do with Jonah? There is no evidence in the book of Jonah that God commented on Jonah's virtue. However, let's look at the story closely and address this question.

First, where was Jonah at the high point of the storm? To give us context, the sailors had thrown all the cargo overboard, prayed to their pagan gods to spare them, and admitted that the ship was about to break in half.

Second, they looked around and asked, "Where's Jonah? Why isn't he with us?" In the midst of the wind, rain, and waves that were so high they were swamping the ship, Jonah was not to be found. I imagine they felt he might have gone overboard.

Of course, looking for any man on deck in a storm was jeopardizing their own lives. To move from one location to another, a sailor had to cling to ropes, and even then it wasn't safe. If a wave came over the bow and hit the sailor hard enough, it could break his grip. Again, the Scriptures don't elaborate on these finer points of the storm, but readers can fill in the gaps of how the crew might have reacted.

Third, another vital piece of information we are not given is that we cannot see, feel, taste, or smell the storm. Think of being soaked head to toe down to your bones by the ice-cold sea—wave after wave seeking to drown you, forcing salt water into your lungs.

You have no time to take a needed gulp of air. The ferocious waves hit you so hard that some of your clothes are torn from your body. You are in a life-and-death battle for survival that you are ill equipped to win.

Want to Get the Most out of Life?

All this time while you gag and attempt to breathe, you hurl vile curses at the elements, since you feel as if you are freezing to death. Your ears are constantly flooded by the sounds of the screaming wind, tearing sails, and boards being ripped from the deck. What about the screams of the crew crying to their pagan gods for mercy, while others wail because they believe they won't see their wives or children again?

Fourth, the captain went below deck, half expecting Jonah to have already been swept overboard. But lo and behold, Jonah was fast asleep as though it were a spring day and he were on a sightseeing cruise. Scripture states that he fell into a deep sleep. He seemed to be unaware of the destruction of life and limb above deck. I can imagine the anger in the captain's voice as he asked Jonah what he was doing down below deck when a storm raged all around them. His question was probably peppered with salty words sailors use that I won't repeat.

Blinking as though waking from a peaceful nap, I imagine Jonah wondered why the captain was so enraged. Maybe the captain grabbed Jonah by the shoulders and gave him several hard shakes, then ordered him to go above deck and join the other crew members.

I can see Jonah stumbling up the steps, gradually becoming aware that the boat was rocking violently and there was water everywhere. He grabbed hold of the rails to secure his balance and was drenched as a huge, cold wave crashed onto the deck. Now he was completely awake and aware of their precarious plight. The whole crew believed they were about to die. To determine who was at fault, they cast lots and the blame fell on Jonah.

Sixth, while trying to balance on the deck, Jonah had no reservation about expressing to the sailors who he was and what God he worshiped. He boldly and confidently stated these words, maybe even in a preaching tone: "I am a Hebrew and I worship the Lord, the God of heaven, who made the sea and the land" (Jonah 1:9).

What a proclamation! Jonah chose an odd place and time to preach a brief sermon, to proclaim his God is above all gods. Jonah was a man with an attitude—a little blunt, but the crew knew where he stood. They had not asked him for details of his Jewish pedigree. All they wanted was enough information to stop the storm.

And yet this is what Jonah did. In my opinion, if any of those sailors bore the slightest ill will toward Jonah for sleeping below deck during the storm, it all disappeared in a puff of smoke. I would also bet that if you and I were there, we would have seen them all temporarily forget the storm and fixate their eyes on Jonah. Their mouths probably gaped open and time stopped. In that moment, there was no storm, no rain, and no ship splitting in half, but only the power of a proclamation of faith they had never heard before in their lives.

If this ship's crew were not in a storm at sea but were attending a big tent revival meeting of today, they all would have stepped forward to be baptized. They may have even seen the heavens open up and witnessed what they thought were angels. Obviously I have no idea about the specifics, but I do know their hearts and minds were changed forever, as they must have been awestruck.

And how do I know this? Because in humility and surrender they asked Jonah what they should do to survive the storm. Jonah very pragmatically said to throw him overboard. Again, I want you to read Jonah's exact words: "Pick me up and throw me into the sea, . . . and it will become calm. I know that it is my fault that this great storm has come upon you" (Jonah 1:12).

These men recognized Jonah as someone special because he was willing to sacrifice his life for their salvation. Does that remind you of someone else? The only sin they were aware of was that Jonah had run away from his God: "They knew he was running away from the Lord, because he had already told them so" (Jonah 1:10b).

Jonah's Two Unparalleled Virtues

Jonah had two unparalleled attributes that most followers of God—in both the Old and New Testaments—did not possess to the extent Jonah did. He placed his life on the line and he had an unwavering faith in God.

Want to Get the Most out of Life?

First, Jonah placed his life on the line. In this story of Jonah running away from God's commission, Jonah placed his life on the line twice. The first time was after the storm ravaged the ship. In this near catastrophe, we learn he had told the sailors before they set sail that he was running from God. What I find interesting is that a superstitious lot of sailors had not refunded his money when he informed them he was running from his God. Perhaps they thought he was a crackpot. Or maybe it never entered their minds that God would cause a storm to sink the ship. Perhaps they were callous to any religion and had become spiritually immune over the years of working in such a harsh environment where life was cheap.

There could be any number of reasons why the sailors didn't expel Jonah from the ship before they began their journey. Regardless, he was laying his life on the line. He strikes me as an exceptionally honest and truthful man because he didn't know what their reaction would be once he told them. However, he informed them as a matter of course. There is another great example of his honesty. When the lot fell on him as the cause of the storm, he accepted the responsibility and gladly stepped forward to be sacrificed.

Jonah told them to pick him up and throw him into the sea because the storm was his fault. Once he was off the ship, the storm would subside. How many people did these sailors know who would willingly give their lives for strangers? This self-sacrificial devotion to duty must have gone against their natural instincts. We can surmise this because when Jonah urged them to throw him overboard, the sailors tried rowing the boat to shore instead. But the storm grew worse, so the sailors followed Jonah's suggestion.

I want to pause here for a moment. We have already seen a word picture of the storm I drew earlier. However, now these men must have been exhausted because of having fought to stay alive for an undisclosed period of time. They were emotionally, physically, and psychologically on their last legs, willing to do anything to keep their ship afloat. But I bet they never anticipated that in order to keep their ship on the surface of the water, they would have to sacrifice a life.

The crew was drenched with wave after wave and they could barely stand on weak knees. I would imagine that their ability to hold any object of weight with exhausted arms was almost gone. Yet I can see each one who did grab Jonah, crying like babies, probably feeling guilty for murder. Some hesitated, some shouted out that there must be another way. One may have even yelled, "God forgive us!"

The men who threw Jonah over the side watched him vanish as he quickly disappeared beneath the waves. In the blink of an eye, the man who had sailed with them was gone.

But in that abysmal moment, the storm subsided, the waves died, and the ocean was calm again. All the men must have rushed to the side of the boat where Jonah had been cast into the sea to perhaps glimpse his person for just a split second to say thank you. Yet they knew they could not see Jonah beneath the water.

At this point, the crew probably fell to the deck of the ship to thank God and to rest and regain their strength. They had all been through a conflict of endurance with Mother Nature and thanks to Jonah, they had endured.

Second, Jonah had an unwavering faith in God. Now, the casual reader might challenge this proposition because when Jonah was called to head east to Nineveh, he headed west to Tarshish instead. To understand the complexity of his disobedience, we have to look at a map of the Mediterranean Sea. As I stated earlier, Nineveh was about a five-hundred-mile journey inland and Tarshish was about three thousand miles by sea.

Jonah was a man who believed in God. He had confidence that once God made a decision, he would keep it. Jonah was the ideal candidate for warning Nineveh that if they did not repent, they would perish. Read what David said to his son Solomon, an admonition I believe Jonah practiced when he wasn't running from God: "And you, my son Solomon, acknowledge the God of your father, and serve him with wholehearted devotion and with a willing mind, for the Lord searches every heart and understands every motive behind the thoughts. If you seek him, he will be found by you; but if you forsake him, he will reject you forever" (1 Chr 28:9).

Jonah's problem was that he had a stubborn heart, a pigheaded spirit. However, he was God's best candidate because of his obstinacy. God knew the motives behind Jonah's thoughts.

Here is why Jonah was chosen for his missionary trip to Assyria.

The five-hundred-mile trip on foot would take a long time. Only a man with a strong personality could walk into a pagan city such as Nineveh and preach. What Assyrian would listen to a Jewish prophet? Assyrians boasted of being the greatest nation in the world. Why should they listen to Jonah?

In comparison, the place where Jonah was born barely deserved a dot on the map. Jonah would have walked into Nineveh in dirty, tattered clothes, probably barefoot, as his sandals would have worn out on the journey. He certainly would have been dehydrated and emaciated. Not a pretty picture for making a first impression.

These pagan civilizations expected priests and priestesses to be adorned with fine jewelry and garments. They had servants or slaves to minister to their every need. Many engaged in sexual acts as part of their worship.

Jonah was a revolutionary prophet. He wanted nothing except for the citizens to listen and repent. And priestly sex with men and women for worship was not on his agenda. He was a tough act to follow because he was a man of faith, principle, and honor. He wasn't a religious sideshow with an angle. I would imagine the local pagan priests and priestesses were raging with jealousy but not envy. Envy requires a desire to possess and be like the one envied. They had too much of a good gig to change.

Yet God knew that Jonah had the tenacity, the boldness, and the unshakable faith no force on earth could stop—the only exception being himself. I also believe God knew Jonah's heart before he commissioned him to preach to Nineveh. He knew Jonah would balk and take a ship to Tarshish.

I also believe that when God calls someone, he has a purpose for the one called as much as for the task he has commissioned.

God knew Jonah needed this trip to smooth and round off his rough spiritual edges. These edges needed to be filed as much as Nineveh needed God's message. Could God have taken Jonah's life for disobedience? Of course, but God, being the author of patience, wanted Jonah to learn from this trip. Jonah needed to see firsthand what Nineveh needed most—mercy, not justice. And by the end of the book, Jonah sees it and still doesn't like it, but he has also learned obedience.

As I said at the beginning of this chapter, Jonah was a conflicted prophet, but even conflicted prophets learn to serve God.

But during the whole story of Jonah, we see that he trusted in God. How do we know of his trust? In the middle of a storm, he was sound asleep below deck. He was awakened and asked for advice. After the crew drew lots, he rallied the sailors together to throw him overboard to calm the storm. How did Jonah know in both instances that God would preserve his life? We are not told. But if you read Matt 8:23–27, Mark 4:35–41, and Luke 8:22–25 you will find Jesus sleeping below decks of a boat in a vicious storm.

In one instance we have a stubborn, pigheaded, proud prophet who wants a city to be razed to the ground, and in the other scenario a perfect Savior who died for mankind. You cannot find any two men more polar opposite. And yet, here it is in Scripture. Jonah slept because of his faith in God. Jesus slept because of his faith in his Father. Neither of them was worried about the raging storms. Neither was concerned for the boats they were on or their lives. Both knew their God and Father would take care of them.

I believe God chose this prophet because as I mentioned previously, he could see into Jonah's heart. God saw Jonah's unwavering trust. And I believe God searches our hearts and overlooks the bad to find the good. When God discovers the good in our lives, we become aware of it though prayer, worship, and our daily walk with him. These three avenues allow us to connect with God, and by so doing, we will find our purpose in life.

There are many parallels in these two stories—two men in boats during storms. In Matt 12:38–45, Jesus uses the story of Jonah's three days in the belly of a large fish as a witness to the three days Jesus would be in his tomb after his crucifixion. In both events, there are three days and nights in a confined area. One was in a fish's belly and the other in a tomb. Jesus rose from the grave, thus conquering death, and Jonah was regurgitated by the fish to preach the good news of repentance. Jesus died and rose from the dead, whereas Jonah "died" when the sailors thought he had drowned after being thrown overboard.

The point here again is that we read about a conflicted, complicated, disagreeable, common man being used by God to preach repentance to Nineveh. And then later, this same prophet, Jonah, is used by Christ as a sign of his resurrection. It gives me personal hope because if God uses someone like Jonah, then we all can have an expectation that we can be used by God every day. All we need is faith in Jesus.

Salmon the father of Boaz, whose mother was Rahab.

MATTHEW 1:5a

Joseph, the husband of Mary, of whom was born Jesus, who is called Christ.

MATTHEW 1:16

— 6 —

How to Pursue Purpose

Rahab the Harlot, Mother of Jesus

AN INTERESTING STORY EMERGED from the destruction of Jericho that none of the Israelites anticipated. They allowed one woman and her biological family to live after having sacrificed everyone else, including animals. This type of city annihilation is called a *ban*. It was done to punish a city-state's wickedness as an offering to God.

Rahab the harlot pulled a special deal with the spies Joshua sent to explore Jericho because she helped them. Her reward was to be spared from the *ban*, an agreement Joshua honored after Jericho was destroyed. Before we look at more details of this intriguing story, I want to tell you two short stories about two Christian ladies I counseled who led questionable lifestyles. Yet unlike Rahab, they never pursued their God-given purposes during the time these events took place.

Two Stories of Lost Purposes

1. I'm Not Sure What to Do

   I had a lady several years ago who came to see me with a personal problem. Kate was beautiful, close to middle age, and single. She usually dressed professionally, but her skirt was a little shorter than those most female clients wore who came to the church counseling program. She came a couple of times, then didn't return for about two years.

What I discovered as we talked during the second time was that her problem had not changed. Names and faces of some of the actors in her life had changed, but she had the same boyfriend.

Without going into detail, she'd had a very tough upbringing and not much family support. This lack of nurture caused her to fend for herself. Kate also discovered she was beautiful and that men paid attention to her. She did not get into the skin trade or prostitution, but did dabble close to the edge with provocative dancing in nightclubs.

One time she was offered an exorbitant fee to model lingerie, but found that the experience made her feel uncomfortable. No matter how respectably it was billed, it was, at heart, an hour of ocular feasting for the men. "The eye never has enough seeing, or the ear its fill of hearing" (Eccl 1:8).

Kate was still involved with Danny, the married man she'd been with at our last meeting. It seems that his marriage was over, but he had not pursued a divorce. He was a little older than Kate and financially stable. Whenever they met for a weekend getaway, she traveled first class and he paid for everything. She had a job and took care of herself, but she could never afford the things he offered on their extravagant excursions.

Our discussion revealed that Kate was still vexed about what to do with her life. She knew their relationship was not sanctioned by the Bible and was not seeking justification. Kate was also experienced enough to know that she could be arm candy for Danny along with what she provided in "room service."

Kate never admitted she was madly in love. Danny professed that he loved her, but she was unsure about how she felt. Other men had lied to her in the past, so she also didn't know if she could trust Danny.

"What should I do?"

My response to her questions was a question: "Has anything changed since our meeting two years ago?"

When she said no, I politely told her she knew the answer and had known the answer for a long time.

We reviewed the solution together. For both Dan and Kate, the best outcome would be for Kate to break off the relationship until he could make up his mind. He needed to either return to his wife or divorce. Until such time, Kate should lead a separate life because the longer she delayed, the more difficult it would be to break off their relationship.

It was very difficult for Kate to issue this ultimatum because the two of them were now over two years into their romantic relationship. We prayed that God would lead them both to make the right choice.

Here's what I have learned about cases of adultery in general, without stereotyping or judging. Most woman will become accustomed to a periodic champagne weekend indulgence on a wealthy patron's gold coin. This artificial, romantic arrangement provides the ecstasies of a playpen without the responsibilities of a crying baby.

It also assumes that the man and woman will set boundaries on allowing themselves to form long-term attachments. You might say that this arrangement is more like sophisticated "friends with benefits." This sweet deal between champagne and beer will end in disaster. Sooner rather than later, the woman will want the permanence of a baby in a bassinet.

When a woman has even a limited background employing her body professionally or semi-professionally in the skin trade, she will soon find it easier and easier to ply her skills. She cannot help herself as she slips into the gestures and movements of being alluring.

Then the man with whom she is involved becomes addicted and chooses not to abandon his drug. Now the two people are trapped by the dysfunctional circumstances of their creation. This entrapment leaves them incapable of thinking rationally about love and responsibility.

2. Tight Jeans

Several years ago, Olivia came for counseling through the church-sponsored program where I had an office. She was about forty and very attractive. For each session we had, she wore tight jeans, which seemed to me more of a sexual message than a means of comfort in our hot Texas climate.

During the first session, she told me she was dissatisfied with her current lifestyle of dancing in a nightclub. Olivia had no education beyond high school, so I suggested she enroll in basic freshman courses at a local junior college. Through our discussion, I leaned she had the intellect along with the ability to pursue academic and professional change. Olivia agreed to enroll in college, and we were set to discuss her progress in our next session.

Olivia was inconsistent in attending counseling. When she did return, she reported that she did not enroll because she needed a babysitter and they were too expensive. She also admitted that she could earn more money dancing two or three nights a week than she could at any other job. I did not see her again for about year, but when she came for a session, she hadn't changed anything in her life.

I believe what happened with Olivia and other woman like her is that unless they have a passion to change and are willing to bear the consequences, their lives will remain the same. "Suppose one of you wants to build a tower. Will he not first sit down and estimate the cost to see if he has enough money to complete it? For if he lays the foundation and is not able to finish it, everyone who sees it will ridicule him, saying, 'This fellow began to build and was not able to finish'" (Luke 14:28–30).

How to Pursue Purpose

A Funny Thing Happened on the Way to Destroy Jericho

A few years ago, my wife and I went on a three-week tour of Israel. It was one of the most exhausting trips I've ever made. On a side note, there didn't seem to be any flat ground in the country. We walked up and down hills or steps all day!

One of the stops we made was at the city of Jericho. Since I had studied about Jericho in seminary and in ancient history classes in college and graduate school, I was really excited about this visit. Personally, I was disappointed when we walked up to the mound of rubble that was the ancient site of Jericho. Without our guide and the posted signs of what had been excavated, I doubt anyone would have been able to tell one pile of stones from another. For me, the wonder and mystery diminished with each step. Maybe I expected too much from the excavation of one of the oldest cities of antiquity. Jericho has a documented history of at least eleven thousand years of occupation.

We were taken on a tour around the outside of the ancient city, but were not permitted to enter due to ongoing excavations and the danger of falling stones. Since the site has been occupied for so many years, the actual wall that surrounded Jericho in Old Testament times had not been identified as of our visit. But I remember pausing for a few minutes in front of the area where our guide indicated that the city gate may have stood in Rahab's time. The story of Rahab, prostitute or inn keeper, was in the forefront of my mind.

I tried to think back over how the city might have looked. The Israelite spies sneaked into the city and entered Rahab's house. The king of Jericho found out and sent his soldiers after them. She hid them on the roof of her house under stalks of flax and told the soldiers they had left the city already. The house Rahab lived in was part of the city wall and had a window on the outside of the wall. Walls around many cities back then were wide enough for a chariot to ride on top and for people to live inside them.

What about the spies? They had to be swift of foot when Rahab lowered them out the window on a scarlet rope. The two men had to hightail it into the surrounding desert and hide for three days near the foothills around the River Jordan. After the coast was clear, they could quietly return to their million-person Israelite camp and report to Joshua.

What was the level of confidence between the two spies and Rahab when they cut their deal? Could either party rely on the other's integrity? I bet that if Rahab had revealed the spies' presence, she would have been richly rewarded in gold. However, if the spies had been captured, a special death would have been planned for Rahab when Israel sacked the city. After all, a *ban* had been planned for Jericho.

But the spies believed Rahab because of her words: "I know that the Lord had given this land to you and that a great fear of you has fallen on us, so that all who live in this country are melting in fear because of you" (Josh 2:9). She added more ammunition to her cause:

> "For the Lord your God is God in heaven above and on the earth below. Now then, please swear to me by the Lord that you will show kindness to my family, because I have shown kindness to you. Give me a sure sign that you will spare the lives of my father and mother, my brothers and sisters, and all who belong to them—and that you will save us from death." "Our lives for your lives!" the men assured her. "If you don't tell what we are doing, we will treat you kindly and faithfully when the Lord gives us the land." (Josh 2:11–14)

The plan was to leave a scarlet rope hanging from the outer window of Rahab's house, marking her home along the wall. The Israelite army was told to spare everyone who was in the room where the rope hung.

As Israel destroyed the city of Jericho, the plan was executed perfectly. Joshua chapter 6 details the destruction of the city and documents that the only living souls who survived the slaughter were Rahab and her family.

How to Pursue Purpose

Up Close and Personal with Rahab: A Profile

What I want to do now is to make Rahab a flesh-and-blood person to you. I don't want you to merely read her name on the pages of a Bible or in a book. I want you to know her up close and personal. See her as an acquaintance; smell the intoxication of her perfume as it stuns your nostrils with its sweetness. Shake hands with her and note how soft her skin is—yet paradoxically, how strong her grip.

Do you hear her talking? First in whispered words, then with her eyes as they speak volumes. Watch how men adore her laugh while women are jealous of it. Men seem to focus on her, ignoring the other women in the room. She casts a spell over men as if she were using a seine net, taking them captive so that they are eager to do her smallest bidding.

The men in her company enthusiastically line up to pull out a chair, open a door, offer her a refreshment, or give her a ride home. Now return in your memory to the girl you knew in high school or college who was like her. She was the one all the young men lined up for like ten pins to get her attention. Now with this either stinging or pleasant memory, you've seen Rahab.

Let's get down to biblical facts. Here is what we know about Rahab: She was a prostitute and possibly an innkeeper, or both. There's a theological debate about which of the two professions she had, but most scholars lean toward prostitute. The debate depends on how her name is interpreted from the Hebrew. But since we are interested only in her story, we will stay with the traditional, textual interpretation.

Rahab was probably frugal with her money because she invested in a large-enough place in the city wall to have had several rooms. In order to run her business as a prostitute, she would have needed more than one room—which could have alternatively been rooms for travelers who needed overnight lodging.

We also know that she was single at the time, although we are unsure whether she had a male or female paramour, or both. I know this frankness may seem difficult to digest, but we are dealing with the Canaanite civilization the way it was. Also, it should not be shocking because of what our own culture has promoted in extended sexual practices. However, back in this time, the Canaanites had gods and goddesses they worshiped. Prostitution was wrapped up in their worship, as we have seen before.

Rahab's parents were alive and she had brothers and sisters who were married, although we are not told whether Rahab had children yet. Scripture tells us that she asked for her extended family to be saved when they gathered in her house, identified by the scarlet cord hanging from her window and extending down the wall.

We are not given important biographical pieces of information such as her age, how long she had been a prostitute, or which gods and goddesses she worshiped. We are also not told whether her family lived separately or with her in the city wall. We don't know much about her hotel business either, but we do know she was industrious because she had flax drying on her roof. In biblical times, all clothing was either made from linen or wool. Linen is made from flax. Could Rahab have been in the cloth-making business as well? It was in this flax that the Israelite spies were hidden until she could send the king's soldiers on a merry wild-goose chase.

Now I want to delve into what we can profile about her personal life based on her profession. This is reasonable speculation because sex for money is the same today as it was eleven thousand years ago. First, it is important to remember that Rahab is of the thirty-first generation in the family line to Jesus Christ. In a biblical sense, because she is in Jesus's genealogical line due to her later marriage to Salmon, she is considered a mother to Jesus.

In much of history, the "blue blood" of royalty is guarded and protected as if those of royal descent had different blood, noble blood. Potential non-royal sons- and daughters-in-law have been executed, imprisoned, or paid off because the royalty believed marriage to a commoner was a contamination of pure, royal blood. But Jesus blew that theory out of the water by boldly proclaiming a prostitute as part of his genealogical heritage (Matt 1:5).

How to Pursue Purpose

Doesn't this unequivocal frankness express without reservation a unique love for the depressed, the poor, the socially rejected, the diseased, the outcast, the deaf, the blind, the lame, and the mentally challenged? Does it not herald from the voices of angels in heaven that Jesus came to earth for those whom society rejects? Jesus doesn't care about whose mother or father spawned a soul. In Christ's vision, the only pedigree is mankind itself, because we all are equal in his eyes because all have the same blood.

Rahab's Pursuit of Purpose

There are two ways of assessing Rahab's lifestyle as a prostitute. We can assume personality traits and characteristics about her and her choice of lifestyle based on what we know of the profession today. She might have been beautiful, and at some point in her pubescence, she learned that men of all ages paid attention to her. As this awareness increased, Rahab began to understand her influence over men. Why not turn that into a business? Consider another scenario. Young Rahab could have been sexually abused, and as still occurs today, she might have turned to selling herself as a way of compensating for low self-esteem and lack of confidence.

Another possibility is that prostitution wasn't considered immoral by Rabab's countrymen. As we have discussed, the pagans had priests and priestesses who where temple prostitutes. It stands to reason that prostitutes might have been found in all levels of society.

Obviously, we don't know how or why Rahab entered this profession, but she seems to have been respected in Jericho, since the king knew of her. She had a large house, albeit built into the wall, which may or may not have been a positive location.

I believe that when Rahab the harlot met the spies, she was in a spiritual abyss. She had heard about the great feats of Jehovah, from the parting of the Red Sea to the defeat of every enemy the Israelites faced. The spies didn't realize that there was a twofold divine agenda in their meeting. First, Rahab protected them so they could report back to Joshua, thus escaping their potential captors. Second, in this meeting they offered Rahab what she had been searching for throughout her life. I think she wanted spiritual freedom because she knew the gods of Jericho were nothing but wood and stone. She received a taste of the real God, Jehovah, in her interaction with the spies and their promise to protect her life when Israel destroyed Jericho.

"'For I know the plans I have for you,' declares the Lord, 'plans to prosper you and not to harm you, plans to give you hope and a future'" (Jer 29:11).

Rahab, an Example of Pursuing Purpose

How can I use Rahab as a great example of one who pursues purpose? After all, look at her. She was a prostitute! That is exactly why I chose her. Although many prostitutes had high standing in ancient society, they were still at the beck and call of other people, either in a religious sense or in a secular arena. Knowing what I know through my counseling experience, I can't help but believe that even women in these ancient times may have felt that they abandoned their self-respect every day they participated in prostitution.

However, with Rahab we see a woman who never gave up. She clung to her passion like many injured athletes do. Some athletes are told they will never compete again. Then to prove medical predictions wrong, they exercise hard and come back, and not only compete but also win. This choice for purpose in life is what Rahab accomplished.

An indicator of this determination is that as well as being a prostitute, she could have been a private innkeeper. On a side note, Josephus (an ancient historian) and other early sources refer to Rahab as an innkeeper. How many women at that time had enough self-discipline and determination to enter a competitive public service industry? She was a woman, and women had no value or rights except for childbearing and keeping the home. And yet she turned her nose up at society, defying their judgment of her and proving them wrong.

How to Pursue Purpose

I believe that Rahab knew from the hard knocks of life that there was something better. Yes, something better—not of this mortal life but in the spiritual realm. Like every human, her soul and heart told her it existed. "He has made everything beautiful in its time. He has also set eternity in the hearts of men; yet they cannot fathom what God has done from beginning to end" (Eccl 3:11).

God sees people like Rahab and, because he loves them, provides a way of escape. "He gives strength to the weary and increases the power of the weak" (Isa 40:29). This is why two New Testament writers commend Rahab's faith. First, in the book of Hebrews: "By faith the prostitute Rahab, because she welcomed the spies, was not killed with those who were disobedient" (Heb 11:31). Her faith was so powerful that some would say she betrayed her people, but she didn't betray anyone. She put her faith in God, which in her case may have meant that she went against her own people.

Her stance of faith against her own people is confirmed in what the apostle James wrote: "In the same way, was not even Rahab the prostitute considered righteous for what she did when she gave lodging to the spies and sent them off in a different direction? As the body without the spirit is dead, so faith without deeds is dead" (Jas 2:25–26).

In closing this chapter, I want to review. I specifically used the case studies of Kate and Olivia became they are examples of how women can gradually slip into these questionable industries and before they know it, they are stuck in the lifestyle. Women who are abused and abandoned from early on in life may not become a prostitute. And most never gravitate to anything resembling the industry. But they all have one character trait in common. Unlike Rahab, they abandon a dream of pursuing a purpose and accept what life has dished out without fighting back. If you see yourself reflected in this chapter, remember that you don't have to live an unfulfilled life. Be like Rahab—hold onto the dream of what God has placed in your heart and pursue your purpose.

"So do not fear, for I am with you; do not be dismayed, for I am your God. I will strengthen you and help you; I will uphold you with my righteous right hand" (Isa 41:10).

Choosing a Purpose without God Will Not Succeed

"I know, O Lord, that a man's life is not his own; it is not for man to direct his steps. Correct me, Lord, but only with justice—not in your anger, lest you reduce me to nothing" (Jer 10:23–24).

I recall as a young man of eighteen just out of high school that I had no idea what I wanted to be and do in life. I barely made a C average in high school. I was a mediocre football jock who played left tackle throughout high school. I received a scholarship at a small university, but halfway through my senior year, I was double tackled and blew out my right knee. Goodbye scholarship.

I was a sort of hero after I left the hospital and returned to classes, especially on Friday nights at the remaining games of the football season. Several girls suddenly noticed me as I hobbled out on the field with the team. But my five seconds of fame got me nowhere with the girls. I learned later that they were acknowledging me publicly for their own five seconds of fame because they were on the cheerleader squad. Raging hormones blind a male's fragile eighteen-year-old ego fairly well.

I enrolled in a local junior college because it was easier to be accepted with my low grades. However, I didn't last long. I promptly bailed out of my classes in less than six weeks and joined the Marines. Since I had passed every prerequisite except the physical, I shaved my head, said goodbye to my folks on a Friday morning, and was ready to leave for the San Diego Marine Depot at noon that same day.

All went well until a fly in the ointment wiggled its way into my military dreams. I failed my physical because of my banged-up knee. Now what was I to do? I'd told everyone I knew I was off to join the Marines. That afternoon when I showed up at home and explained what had happened to my parents, they expressed great relief. It was October 1969. They had resigned themselves to the fact that they would not see me alive again. The war in Vietnam was at a fever pitch, and young Marines were being chewed up and spit out like fresh meat in a butcher's grinder.

My only disconcerting recourse was to reenroll in the junior college and eat crow when I saw my old friends. I changed my major three times and transferred to three other colleges, burning up my Dad's saving account. Ultimately, at age twenty, I was baptized. I learned years later that my father, being a product of the Great Depression and having served in the Marines during WWII, was on the verge of kicking me out of our house. My stepmother intervened after my baptism and asked him to give me a last chance. She could tell I'd changed my outlook on life.

Choosing God's Purpose in Prayer

I began praying for God's will in my life and admitted I had no clue what to do, but in the interim I took a few elective Bible courses and made As for the first time in my life. I then announced I wanted to transfer to a Christian college and prepare to be a missionary. I won't bore you with extensive details, but in January 1972, I met a young lady at the Christian college and we married in December. And guess what? She was from Rhodesia, Africa. Now I had a place to go as a missionary.

I had been accepted on probation, but I worked hard and improved my grades significantly. Then I applied for entrance to a theological graduate school and was accepted. By December of 1974, my wife had earned her master's degree in special education. She supported us while I studied and finally graduated with my master's degree. In August 1975, we were off to her home in Rhodesia, Africa.

I offer this short story from so long ago because I struggled very hard to find my way with God as my leader. I was impetuous, impulsive, and thoughtless, and worked hard to make *my* choices become reality. And even today after having retired, I still struggle—as many of you do too—because it's never easy to allow God to lead us in our quests.

Want to Get the Most out of Life?

How to Pray for Purpose

"For none of us lives to himself alone and none of us dies to himself alone. If we live, we live to the Lord; and if we die, we die to the Lord. So, whether we live or die, we belong to the Lord" (Rom 14:7–8).

It took me a long time—longer than I care to admit—to realize that while pursuing my quest, I needed to be in daily prayer asking for God's guidance. In reality, he already knows the course of our lives. "Show me, O Lord, my life's end and the number of my days; let me know how fleeting is my life. You have made my days a mere handbreadth; the span of my years is as nothing before you. Each man's life is but a breath" (Ps 39:4–5). However, when we finally realize we can give the burden of a quest to God, it makes our pursuit much easier.

"The Lord foils the plans of the nations; he thwarts the purposes of the peoples. But the plans of the Lord stand firm forever, the purposes of his heart through all generations" (Ps 33:10–11). The best daily practice is to get on your knees and pray, "Thy will be done in my life." "Wait for the Lord; be strong and take heart and wait for the Lord" (Ps 27:14).

How can I know that what I ask of God is his will? How do I know he hears me? John gives us the answer: "I write these things to you who believe in the name of the Son of God so that you may know that you have eternal life. This is the assurance we have in approaching God: that if we ask anything *according to his will*, he hears us. And if we know that he hears us—whatever we ask—we know that we have what we asked of him" (1 John 5:13–15, italics added).

From this passage we can infer that if what we ask of God is not his will, then he does not hear us. Does this mean he does not hear our prayer? Certainly not. This phrase is used in the sense that if we ask something that is not of his will, then it's as if God delays his answer because he knows we are not ready to receive it.

Let me provide a personal example. As I have written earlier, I have not been the paragon of virtue in regards to the topic of this book. But when I have followed through, in *God's* time and not mine, my request worked out better than I could have imagined. The times where it appeared to me that God did not hear my request, the result was in my best interest anyway.

After ten years of having a private counseling practice, I decided I wanted to shift the emphasis of my work to going out to emergency situations and counseling on the scene of accidents, robberies, or natural disasters. I also wanted to work from home and not have the overhead expenses of an office. How did I do this? I began praying every day about my desire, as I didn't know what else to do. After a couple of years, I thought God had not heard my prayers and that my request was not of his will.

During the following year, I received numerous calls to go to places all over Texas to counsel after disasters, such as a fire at an oil refinery where a large number of people died; a company where a huge explosion resulted in employee deaths; and several bank robberies after which (although no one was shot) the employees were traumatized.

In God's time frame, I also received calls to go out of state. I went to New Orleans for two weeks after Hurricane Katrina, and to New York City for a week after the September 11 disaster. There were several other trips, but the most memorable was a two-week stint in Kabul, Afghanistan.

Although I was excited to travel and believe I did help the people I counseled, I was spending too much time away from my wife. She never displayed her fear, but I knew she worried every time I went overseas to a dangerous zone. Time for a new goal for me and my counseling work. My new quest was to counsel in an office setting where I didn't pay the overhead and was not responsible for billing insurance companies for payment. Then I went to the Scriptures to guide me in my own personal quest.

"Morning by morning, O Lord, you hear my voice; morning by morning I lay my requests before you and wait in expectation" (Ps 5:3).

"Show me your ways, O Lord, teach me your path; guide me in your truth and teach me, for you are God my Savior, and my hope is in you all day long" (Ps 25:4–5).

Just two more Scriptures as I lay a foundation for the conclusion.

"For he will command his angels concerning you to guard you in all your ways; they will lift you up in their hands, so that you will not strike your foot against a stone. You will tread upon the lion and the cobra; you will trample the great lion and the serpent" (Ps 91:11–13).

"A man's steps are directed by the Lord. How then can anyone understand his own way?" (Prov 20:24).

There are so many other scriptures the Lord gave to guide me in my quests, but these will be adequate. A year later, I was on assignment at a military base in Hawaii, counseling troops who had returned from Iraq. I received a phone call that changed my life—an offer for the job as an onsite EAP counselor! That is where I spent the last twelve years of my career, in a job that was never onerous and where I learned more than I did during my graduate studies.

If you desire your quest to be successful, here is my best advice: Don't depend upon yourself. The Bible has all the answers. "Many are the plans in a man's heart, but it is the Lord's purpose that prevails" (Prov 19:21).

"In his heart a man plans his course, but the Lord determines his steps" (Prov 16:9).

Thank you for reading this book. I pray it will be helpful in your own personal quest.

www.ingramcontent.com/pod-product-compliance
Lightning Source LLC
Chambersburg PA
CBHW071331190426
43193CB00041B/1494